WRITERS AND THEIR W

ISOBEL ARMSTRONG
General Editor

J. G. FARRELL

photograph by Michael Leonard

J. G. FARRELL

J. G. FARRELL

John McLeod

© Copyright 2007 by John McLeod
First published in 2007 by Northcote House Publishers Ltd,
Horndon, Tavistock, Devon, PL19 9NQ, United Kingdom.
Tel: +44 (0) 1822 810066   Fax: +44 (0) 1822 810034.

All rights reserved. No part of this work may be reproduced or stored in an information retrieval system (other than short extracts for the purposes of review) without the express permission of the Publishers given in writing.

British Library Cataloguing-in-Publication Data
A catalogue record for this book is available from the British Library

ISBN 978-0-7463-1055-7 hardcover
ISBN 978-0-7463-0986-5 paperback
Typeset by PDQ Typesetting, Newcastle-under-Lyme
Printed and bound in the United Kingdom

For Linda

Contents

Acknowledgements viii

Biographical Outline ix

List of Abbreviations xi

1 Introduction: 'fanciful tales'   1

2 The Early Novels   11

3 Ireland, 1919–1921   34

4 India, 1857 & 1871   56

5 Singapore, 1937–1942   79

6 Critical Legacy   97

Notes 105

Bibliography 111

Index 114

Acknowledgements

I must thank Richard Brown, Shirley Chew and Alistair Stead, under whose guidance I first studied J. G. Farrell, for introducing me to a writer whose work has come to shape so much of my engagement with the novel in English. I am also indebted to my fellow Farrell enthusiasts, especially Ralph Crane, Glenn Hooper, Daniel Lea, and Peter Morey, who have kindly shared with me their work on Farrell over the years and have corresponded enjoyably about our shared passion for Farrell's writing. All scholars of Farrell owe a major obligation to his biographer, Lavinia Greacen, and I am personally in her debt for the help she has given me at several stages of this book. I would also like to thank Weidenfeld and Nicolson (a division of Orion Books) for permission to quote from copyright materials. All quotations from *Troubles* are copyright © 1970 J. G. Farrell, and reproduced by permission of the author c/o Rogers, Coleridge & White Ltd., 20 Powis Mews, London W11 1JN.

My colleagues in the School of English, University of Leeds, remain a constant source of support, friendship and entertainment: especially Mark Batty, Tracy Hargreaves, Graham Huggan, Francis O'Gorman and Andrew Warnes. My friends Rachel Evans, Rick Jones, Alex Nield, and Martin Rushworth have offered welcome distraction on too many occasions to mention. I am especially grateful to Julie Adams for stimulation and affection, her generous and insightful comments on my early drafts, and her valuable support in bringing this book to fruition.

My parents, Veronica and James McLeod, are my inspiration, as too are my sister Linda and her family: Brian, Caitlin, Lydia and Madeleine. This book is for Linda, with love.

John McLeod
De Vergulde Gaper
Amsterdam

Biographical Outline

1935	Born James Gordon Farrell, January 25, in Liverpool, to an Irish mother and English father.
1947	The Farrells move to Dublin.
1948–53	Boards at Rossall public school in Fleetwood, Lancashire; returns to Ireland during the holidays.
1955	Travels to Canada and works briefly in the Arctic.
1956	Begins undergraduate studies at Brasenose College, Oxford, reading Law; in December becomes seriously ill with polio and is confined to an iron lung; makes only a partial recovery and permanently loses some mobility in his upper body.
1957–60	Recommences undergraduate studies at Brasenose College, but changes to reading Modern Languages (French and Spanish); graduates with a Third.
1960	Moves to France and works as a teacher; begins to write.
1963	First novel, *A Man From Elsewhere*, published as part of Hutchinson's New Authors series.
1965	Second novel, *The Lung*, published; moves to London.
1966	Finishes third novel, *A Girl in the Head*, which is accepted for publication; awarded Harkness Fellowship which funds two years of graduate study in the United States; moves to New Haven and studies at Yale University; begins work on *Troubles*.
1968–9	Returns to London; completes *Troubles*; begins regular reviewing for the *Spectator*.
1970	*Troubles* published in December to critical acclaim.
1971	*Troubles* awarded the Faber Memorial Prize in May; travels extensively in India.
1973	*The Siege of Krishnapur* awarded the Booker Prize for

	fiction; during the acceptance speech he condemns Booker's exploitative practices in the Far East.
1975	Travels to Singapore and Vietnam to research his next novel.
1978	Sixth and last full-length novel, *The Singapore Grip*, published.
1979	Moves to Bantry Bay, Ireland, in March; begins work on another India novel; on August 11 is washed out to sea and drowned while fishing just yards from his home; his body is recovered from the sea a month later; buried at the St James Church of Ireland, Durrus.
1981	Posthumous publication of unfinished novel, *The Hill Station*, together with his 1971 'Indian Diary', two appreciations and a personal memoir.

Abbreviations

Abbreviations (in order of first publication)

ME   *A Man From Elsewhere* (London: New Authors Limited, 1963).
L   *The Lung* (1965; London: Corgi, 1967).
GH   *A Girl in the Head* (1967; London: Pan Books, 1969).
T   *Troubles* (1970; London: Flamingo, 1984).
SK   *The Siege of Krishnapur* (1973; London: Flamingo, 1985).
SG   *The Singapore Grip* (1978; London: Flamingo, 1984).
HS   *The Hill Station: an unfinished novel and an Indian Diary* (with Two Appreciations and a Personal Memoir), ed. by John Spurling (1981; London, Flamingo, 1987).

1

Introduction: 'fanciful tales'

'One day we shall vanish. But for the moment how lovely we are!'
(*T* 329)

On 15 June 1978, a letter appeared in the *New York Review of Books* which called upon the Kenyan Government to release the distinguished writer Ngugi wa Thiong'o, who had been imprisoned under Kenya's Public Security Act following the publication of his novel *Petals of Blood* (1978). Its signatories included several major figures from the world of literature: James Baldwin, Margaret Drabble, Edna O'Brien, Harold Pinter, Philip Roth, and the novelist J. G. Farrell.[1] Farrell's presence in this list reveals not only his often passionate engagement with affairs, both past and present, in countries with a history of British colonialism, but also that his reputation and status as a writer of significance had been firmly established by the late 1970s. He had worked hard and had overcome many challenges in securing his career and renown as a novelist. Like Ngugi he took his vocation very seriously as a writer unafraid to challenge authority, prejudice and exploitation. By the latter part of the decade Farrell's novels had established him as a major figure in contemporary literature. A busy and productive future, surely, lay in wait for him.

Farrell's three novels of the 1960s had attracted modest attention, but it was his writing of the 1970s which transformed his life and career. *Troubles* (1970) won the Geoffrey Faber Memorial Prize, while *The Siege of Krishnapur* (1973) was awarded the prestigious Booker Prize for fiction. He became a reviewer for leading publications such as the *Spectator*, *Listener*, *New Stateman* and the *Times Literary Supplement*, and in June 1978 was just about to publish his longest and most ambitious novel,

The Singapore Grip (1978), which, with the two preceding novels, formed the 'Empire Trilogy', for which he is best remembered.

The Trilogy may be thought of as a loose confederation of works, linked not by a common plot or cast of characters (although the figure of the Major from *Troubles* appears again in *The Singapore Grip*) but rather by a shared set of historical, political and literary concerns. Farrell described it as a triptych 'with each panel presenting a picture of the Empire at a different historical watershed and by their association shedding, I hope, some light on each other', but the term 'Trilogy' has stuck.[2] Characterised by the humane yet unswervingly critical rendering of British colonialism, and stylistically innovative in its ironic and often surreal engagement with the genre of the historical novel, the Trilogy constitutes a ground-breaking act of creativity in the history of post-war fiction. In John Spurling's words, 'The influence of [Farrell's] uniquely up-to-date mixture of black humour, surrealism and liberal-left disapproval of lingering romanticism about the British Empire can still be detected in a later generation of novelists'.[3] In my view, the Empire Trilogy must be considered as a vital influence on a new generation of postcolonial novelists who emerged in the 1980s: Timothy Mo, Salman Rushdie, Kazuo Ishiguro, Amitav Ghosh, and others.[4]

Sadly, Farrell never lived to encounter the work of these writers, nor enjoy at length the life as a leading novelist for which he had worked so long and hard. On Saturday 11 August 1979, he died in tragic circumstances in Bantry Bay, Ireland, where he had moved from London only a few months previously. He had gone fishing near his new home just as a freak and unexpected storm began to pound the coast, and was swept away by the sea's notoriously fierce currents. His attempts to swim to safety would have been hampered by his lack of mobility: as a young man Farrell had been struck down with polio which had affected his ability to use his arms. The incident was witnessed by a nearby family who raised the alarm, but the Irish coastguard could not find him in the rough sea. On 13 September, a month after his disappearance and just over a year after the publication of the letter about Ngugi in the *New York Review of Books*, Farrell's body was discovered washed up in Bantry Bay. The local Coroner recorded a verdict of death by accidental drowning. He was buried in St James's Church of Ireland in Durrus. He was 44 years old.

As Farrell's biographer, Lavinia Greacen, has shown in her fascinating and extremely moving account of his life and work, Farrell's death was keenly felt by his family and close friends, many of whom were fellow writers.[5] Writing in the *Literary Review* in 1979, John Palliser expressed his deep regret at 'the loss to our literature of this extraordinary fertile and complex imagination'.[6] In studying their accounts and memoirs of Farrell, one discovers, not surprisingly, a remarkable and deeply-felt affection for Jim (as he was known) which is still palpable nearly 30 years after his death. In 1997 I attended a conference about Farrell at Royal Holloway, University of London, organised by the scholar Daniel Lea, which was attended by Farrell's mother Jo and his brother Richard, and by several of his friends which included the writers John Spurling and Margaret Drabble. I remember being deeply moved by the levels of fondness and warmth which animated their words. Farrell was still dearly missed. If anything, the passage of time had sharpened the sense of loss felt by those who knew him well. But more surprising, perhaps, is the similarly high degree of affection for Farrell which one discovers amongst his readers, most of whom (like me) have encountered his writing after his death. Indeed, one of the unexpected pleasures of studying Farrell's novels and discussing them with others is the sense that one has joined a community of enthusiasts, not simply critics. Not just his life but his work seems to generate remarkable amounts of affection in Farrell's ever-growing circle of readers. For most readers of his novels, there comes a point where one stops reading the work of J. G. Farrell and starts reading 'Jim' – the name by which Farrell is often known amongst his many admirers, as well as his friends.

The fact of his premature death may give an added poignancy to his writing. When reading Farrell's novels it is hard to forget that his published fiction perhaps represents only a part of what he could have achieved had he lived. But this is not the only reason. As with most writers, the work has a trajectory to a degree independent of its creator. In reading Farrell's fiction we encounter a literary sensibility that mediates brilliantly between historical circumstances and their effects on the emotional and imaginative worlds of those, as Farrell once put it, 'undergoing history'. His unique, generous yet elusive narrative voice readily invites its readers into its fictional worlds, engaging them in an entertaining yet unsettling reading experience.

The relationship between this writer and his work is important and enigmatic. As we shall see, the novel was often a place where Farrell explored and attempted to resolve key events in his life, especially in his (often neglected) early writing. This book is my attempt to explore the significance, achievement and value of Farrell's work in the context of his life, very much in the spirit of critical homage to a writer who should be better known both to general readers and students of literature today.

Ireland was a significant location in Farrell's life, literary career, and unfortunate death. James Gordon Farrell was born in Liverpool on 25 January 1935. His mother, Jo, was Irish with family connections in Dublin, while his father, Bill, was from Liverpool but worked in India and the Far East. After the Second World War, the family moved to Dublin while Farrell attended school in England, eventually boarding at Rossall public school in Fleetwood, Lancashire, between 1948 and 1953 and returning to Ireland in the holidays. It was a peripatetic early life which would leave its mark. Farrell became aware from a young age of the prejudicial character of British attitudes to its erstwhile colonies and those considered as different, and he also grew up with a sense of not comfortably belonging in either Britain or Ireland. As he recalled in an interview in 1978, his travels across the Irish Sea occurred at a time 'when travel arrangements for the Irish were posted on the assumption the Irish were subhuman'.[7] As Caroline Moorehead notes, 'At School he was addressed as an Irish boy; in Ireland he felt English'.[8]

His burgeoning interest in literature was similarly itinerant and characterised by an international flavour, the influence of which would be felt subsequently throughout his novels. His favourite writers included the Anglo-Welsh novelist Richard Hughes and the Polish émigré Joseph Conrad, and he would come to admire Leo Tolstoy. French literature was a particular passion; in a short essay of 1975 he describes his youthful love of the works of the sailor-turned-novelist Pierre Loti (1850–1923) and controversial, prolific writer Colette (1873–1954).[9] He would eventually graduate from Oxford University with a degree in Modern Languages.

Farrell arrived at Brasenose College, Oxford, in October 1956, having spent a short spell working in Canada. He originally enrolled to study Law, and pursued his enthusiasm for rugby as soon as he settled into college life. A strong, athletic and gifted rugby footballer, Farrell excelled in the College leagues. All of this was to change suddenly in November 1956 when he injured his shoulder during a rugby match. A few days later he fell ill and was taken to hospital in a serious condition. He was diagnosed with polio, a potentially deadly virus which attacks the nervous system and can render its sufferers paralysed within hours of infection. Farrell's life was in jeopardy for a number of weeks. He suffered severe paralysis and, because his respiratory system could not function properly (a common effect of polio), he was placed in an iron lung to help him breathe. Although he survived the attack and gradually recovered mobility, the illness irreversibly changed his life and, in many ways, destroyed the athletic, cheerful person he had previously been. Farrell emerged from the illness physically and emotionally fragile, and he never recovered full use of his upper body, especially his right arm. Deeply depressed and troubled by his sudden illness and its consequences, he switched from Law to Modern Languages (French and Spanish) at Oxford, and graduated in 1960.

The impact of Farrell's illness can be discerned throughout his fiction and part of his purpose in writing was to explore and make sense of the dramatic, unanticipated and alarming change which utterly transformed his life. His most explicit engagement with it is found in his second novel, *The Lung* (1965), but in each of his seven published novels illness and its consequences are prevailing issues. Doctors are recurring figures in Farrell's work, while key characters often suffer from debilitating or fatal conditions. Both Monica in *The Lung* and Angela Spencer in *Troubles* have leukaemia, while Dr Dunstable in *The Siege of Krishnapur* succumbs to cholera. As many critics have pointed out, illness as metaphor is a recurring feature of Farrell's writing and shapes his sense of the essential infirmity of human life. In Ronald Binns's words, in Farrell's writing 'human beings and their communities are in perpetual states of siege, battered by circumstance both from within and without'.[10] Above all, the psychological and existential consequences of Farrell's experience of polio reverberate throughout his fiction.

Farrell's first three novels repeatedly feature disillusioned, depressive men, disenchanted with life and gloomily fixated on their inability to form meaningful relationships or take much solace from the world's possibilities. The early books are relentlessly, if not entirely, bleak and open a dispiriting vista on the potential meaninglessness and pain of human life. Even in the Empire Trilogy, in which there is frequently adopted a more comical, ironic and benign attitude to the potential absurdity of existence, the influence of Farrell's illness can be felt. These novels often feature a central character who struggles painfully to confront the sudden disintegration of their entire way of life in the face of unstoppable and impersonal historical circumstances, such as Edward Spencer in *Troubles* or the Collector in *The Siege of Krishnapur*. They are especially compelling figures because they emerge from contrary impulses on the part of their creator. On the one hand, in charting the collapse of their certainties Farrell articulates the theme of the end of Empire and mocks the grandiosity and confidence of the imperious attitudes of Britain's colonial classes. Yet on the other hand, Farrell retains, and is motivated by, a remarkable compassion for their predicament and empathizes greatly with their feelings of bewilderment, helplessness and loss of control. The presence of such compassion has caused less perceptive readers to suggest that Farrell sympathizes with British colonialism in the Empire Trilogy and is nostalgic for its passing. As I shall subsequently argue, this is an unsubtle reading of Farrell's later work which does a major disservice to his achievement as a novelist. It also fails to understand *why* Farrell was writing, at both political and personal levels.

After graduating from Oxford, Farrell moved to France where he worked as a teacher and began to decant his sombre view of the world into fiction. His first novel, *A Man From Elsewhere* (1963) was published as part of the Hutchinson press's New Authors series. Farrell spent much of the 1960s supporting himself by taking a number of teaching jobs, both in Britain and mainland Europe, and working on his skills as a novelist. By the end of the decade he had produced three novels, each with a contemporary setting. *The Lung* was published in 1965, followed by *A Girl in the Head* in 1967. As he was completing the latter, he was successful in applying for a Harkness Fellowship which funded two years of study in the United States, at Yale University. During a stay in New York, Farrell took a ferry to Block Island where he came across the ruin of the Ocean View Hotel. The ruin fired his imagination, and an idea for an historical novel began to form itself. It became the prototype for the Majestic Hotel in *Troubles*, which was published to critical acclaim in 1970.

In turning his attention to the past and exploring a moment of historical significance – in this instance the end of British rule in Ireland in the early 1920s – Farrell discovered fertile ground for his novelistic imagination and chanced upon a much more successful method for articulating many of the issues which preoccupied his early, less successful novels: illness, pain, failure, decline. By subjecting characters from the past history of Empire to daunting and unhappy experiences, Farrell found a way of displacing himself from the dispiriting, leaden pressure of his hitherto gloomy representation of the world and allowed more humorous and ironical attitudes to blossom. The pain and legacy of his illness became transformed, through the act of writing, into a remarkable creative energy which fuelled his attempt as a novelist to write critically about the end of the British Empire. It was as if the historical, public worlds of his later fiction offered him a way of framing and mobilising his unhappy experiences as a young man, turning them into artistic and intellectual resources. The existential bleakness and infrequent sardonic humour of the early novels assumed a new purpose.

Troubles offered a view of the end of Empire in Ireland from a seemingly remote, microcosmic perspective. It plotted the changes to the country through the declining fortunes of the Majestic hotel's owners, the Spencer family; the consciousness of its central figure, the Major; and the hotel's memorable elderly residents. It is an unconventional novel, working ironically with the genre of the historical novel in an attempt to articulate the experience of history felt by those living at a remove from the heart of historical affairs. Although the emphasis often falls upon the fragility and frailty of human life, the novel is frequently comical, bizarre, even absurd – wry melancholy is preferred to onerous dejection. Its successful design and historical focus gave Farrell a method for writing about history which helped him structure and discipline his imagination. Through writing *Troubles*, Farrell discovered his style. The end of the British Empire became the ostensible theme of his fiction for the rest of his life, as he chose deliberately to write critically about the Empire at moments of crisis: events in Ireland, the Indian 'Mutiny' or war of independence in 1857, the fall of Singapore to Japan in February 1942.

Perhaps because of those early experiences crossing between Ireland and Britain, which exposed him to a sense of 'outsiderdom' and displacement, Farrell did not accept political or national structures which denied the humanity of different cultures and peoples. The Empire Trilogy sought to expose and fragment the arrogant self-confidence of British colonialism and the attitudes it created, chiefly by focusing on the decline and fall of Empire from the perspective of the British colonial classes. Although Farrell could never fully articulate the experience of Empire from the perspective of the colonized – the Catholic Irish peasantry, Indian sepoys, the Chinese and others in Malaya – his commitment to contesting the attitudes which kept such peoples in servitude and poverty, especially in *The Singapore Grip*, affords the Empire Trilogy an important political dimension. Arguably, Farrell's innovative style as an historical novelist, combined with his political opposition to the Empire and its legacy that was fuelled by his mounting engagement with Marxian political philosophy, have made him such an inspirational figure for many postcolonial writers.

Troubles was initially only a modest commercial success, but it set Farrell on the trajectory of writing the Empire Trilogy and strengthened his growing critical reputation. By the 1970s he had made his home in London, although he travelled widely. On winning the Geoffrey Faber Memorial Prize in 1971 with *Troubles* he visited India as part of his research for *The Siege of Krishnapur*. Like his previous book, this novel portrayed the Empire ironically at a moment of crisis, coming apart at its seams. A confident and controlled novel, it is perhaps Farrell's funniest – Farrell wryly called it 'just an adventure story dressed up in intellectual pyjamas'.[11] The novel was fiercely scathing of the arrogance, confidence and aggrandisement of Empire, as well as being remarkably amusing in its absurd, almost slapstick representation of the beleaguered colonials marooned in the Residency in the fictional Indian cantonment of Krishnapur.

It was awarded the Booker Prize of 1973, not without some discord (in its early days the Booker Prize judges did not welcome or seek to generate controversy, as they have in more recent years). During his acceptance speech Farrell criticized world capitalism and drew attention to the exploitation of Booker's poorly-paid workers in countries with a history of colonialism. He would be using the money, he informed his audience, to research his next novel which would engage directly with the exploitative practices of big business; the result would be *The Singapore Grip*. Although Farrell did not court publicity and was in many ways a rather private figure, he was unafraid to demonstrate his commitment to those whom he believed were unduly in distress, whether they were plantation workers or fellow novelists.

The years of the 1970s were Farrell's busiest and most successful. In 1975 he used his Booker Prize award to fund a trip to Singapore and Vietnam as part of his research for *The Singapore Grip*, his longest and most self-assured novel, which was published in 1978. The novel was written to a degree from a Marxian-influenced position in its recounting of Singapore's fall to the Japanese in 1942, primarily through the declining fortunes of Blackett and Webb, a large rubber business based in Singapore. The themes of decline, loss of authority and crisis loom large, as expected. But while Farrell's comical approach is clearly evident in the novel, his penchant for the bizarre has perhaps waned a little. It is the most confident and mature of Farrell's novels, and it also reveals the direction of his ongoing development as a writer: some of the melancholic, uncanny atmosphere of the previous books is less in abundance. *The Singapore Grip* seems more comfortable with the genre of the historical novel, especially in its epic proportions, and is closer to conventional notions of the proper subject-matter of history.

A combination of financial and personal motives influenced Farrell to move from London to Bantry Bay in March 1979. At his death he was working on another novel of India, much smaller in scale than *The Singapore Grip*, concerning a hill station in Simla during the late nineteenth century. Two characters from *The Siege of Krishnapur*, Dr and Miriam McNab, were to reappear. After Farrell's death the unfinished draft of the novel was published under the title *The Hill Station* (1981) along with Farrell's 'Indian Diary' and memoirs by his friends. As Lavinia Greacen tells us, Farrell was working on *The Hill Station* for most of the day he died, finishing an important section before pulling on his anorak and leaving his house to go fishing. The last words he wrote were spoken by a character called Potter: 'It's the servants in India, Emily, they spread all sort of fanciful tales' (*HS* 151).

The Empire Trilogy is certainly fanciful in the fullest and best sense of the word: imaginative, fantastical, bizarre, endearing. But it does not trifle with history. Its combination of imaginative adventurousness fused with political and artistic seriousness remains its most remarkable aspect. Like the servant to whom Potter refers, Farrell revelled in making up stories about the Empire, falling somewhere between truth and fiction, which subtly but surely menaced and unnerved the legitimacy of colonialism and its legacy. As his support of Ngugi suggests, Farrell understood that a writer and their work could be subversive and challenge the authority of those in power. His fiction aims to do precisely this, even if (as we shall see) it is not always fully successful.

Let us be clear: Farrell's novels were certainly not akin to the plain tales of Empire which celebrated or justified British colonialism, even if some of his early critics failed to grasp the radical and progressive aspects of his work and dismissed him as stylistically unadventurous or as nostalgic for Empire. As I shall show in the final chapter, in the years following Farrell's death there have been considerable shifts in his critical fortunes, and only in recent years has his legacy been better understood. It is one which is discernible in the works of other distinguished writers: Timothy Mo's *An Insular Possession* (1986), Rohinton Mistry's *Such A Long Journey* (1991), Giles Foden's *Ladysmith* (1999), Matthew Kneale's *English Passengers* (2000) and several others besides, take Farrell's achievement partly as their example and inspiration. It is time to find out why.

2

The Early Novels

Farrell's first novel, *A Man From Elsewhere* (1963), recalls in its title a popular saying: 'A man from elsewhere is a man without a soul' (*ME* 53). As this may suggest, the book is preoccupied with existential questions about the nature, purpose and potential meaninglessness of life. The tone throughout is resolutely depressing and bleak. Farrell was working in France as a teacher while writing the novel, and the influence of his passion for French literature can be discerned throughout. His early writing in general is certainly influenced by existentialist works of such figures as Jean-Paul Sartre and especially Albert Camus, one of Farrell's lifelong favourite writers.

The novel's title echoes Camus's *L'Etranger* (1942) with its emphasis on the outsider figure, and there are several references to Camus's work.[1] The novel is set in the French town of Saint Guilhelm and concerns the conflict between its chief protagonists, Regan and Sayer. Sinclair Regan is a famous novelist and former Communist who quit the party in 1940 during the German occupation of France. Once an influential and inspirational activist, his writings since 1941 have been seen as tantamount to a betrayal of his comrades. At the time of the novel's setting, 1961, Regan is terminally ill, living out his last days in Saint Guilhelm. News circulates that he is about to be awarded the Catholic Prize for World Peace, a prospect which alarms his former colleague Gerhardt who edits a Communist newspaper in Paris, the *Workers' International Review*. Concerned that Regan will be remembered with admiration and sympathy rather than as a betrayer and turncoat, Gerhardt asks one of his journalists, Sayer, to travel to Saint Guilhelm to gather information for an article for the *Review* which will destroy Regan's reputation. As Gerhardt explains, time is of the essence:

'There's a considerable difference between a man who dies in disgrace and a man whose good name is questioned after his death' (*ME* 23). As his name wittily suggests, Sayer will be largely responsible for telling Regan's fortunes to the world.

Sayer travels to Saint Guilhelm and stays with Regan – who is perfectly aware of Gerhardt's motives and Sayer's intentions – where he meets two other important characters: Gretchen, apparently Regan's teenage daughter, and Luc, with whom she has been having an affair. Luc is a frustrated writer of banal film scripts which depict conventional heroic images of brave men fighting in the Second World War. After some digging around, Sayer soon stumbles across a potential scandal. During the war, Regan was a close friend of the Nazi commandant of the occupied village, Heinrich, and had a part to play in betraying a member of the French Resistance who was subsequently executed. Regan gave Heinrich the names of three suspects on the understanding that no action would be taken against them, yet Heinrich broke his word. In a further twist, it emerges that Regan's wife (who is never named) had an affair with Heinrich, and that Gretchen is their child. At the end of the war Heinrich committed suicide, while Regan's wife suffered a breakdown and was sent away to England, where she died shortly afterwards. In the novel's climax, Sayer delivers a tirade of condemnation to Regan about his past and rescues Gretchen from a suicide attempt brought on by Regan's cruel treatment of her (he has refused her access to him in his final hours).

The conflict between Sayer and Regan is between two ultimately discredited versions of freedom which the novel brings equally to crisis: Sayer's Communist advocacy of freedom from economic and class oppression via collective action and proletarian revolt, and Regan's ardent existentialism which grounds human freedom not in doctrinal belief but in individual action: 'it was not the belief that mattered but rather what a man made of himself within the framework of his belief' (*ME* 83).[2] The novel suggests that neither seems remotely fulfilling nor meaningful. Regan's rampant individualism has been at the expense of his relationships with others: his adopted daughter, wife, and erstwhile friends. In his final hours the grandiose designs of his precious philosophizing seem diminished when faced with the certainty of his death, and his final confrontation with Sayer calls into question the worth of his life's work.

Sayer makes Regan regard himself not as a world-famous and inspirational, innovative thinker, but as 'a selfish, brutal old man, obsessed with his own uniqueness and independence' (*ME* 181). Regan may have his philosophies and his prizes, but he has little compassion and is unable to love. Significantly, he only declares his love for Gretchen and the memory of his wife in private – to himself and not to others (*ME* 84). He washes his hands of any responsibility for the wartime executions of the Resistance fighters. According to his individualist philosophy, he believes that Heinrich acted entirely of his own free will in ordering the executions, so Regan considers himself blameless. His last act of 'free will' is the shooting of his dog for no apparent purpose, which underlines the destructive and fascistic possibilities of his existentialism. Sayer condemns him for 'manicuring his own lovely soul' (*ME* 182) instead of paying attention to those around him. That 'soul' has been an illusion and a betrayal. Regan dies a man 'without a soul' in both senses of the phrase: in isolation, and devoid of any redemptive or empathetic qualities.

Farrell is too gloomy to proffer any alternative affirmative possibilities in the novel. Despite his attack on Regan, Sayer is hardly a compassionate or redeeming individual, and certainly is not an alternative positive figure. The novel opens with a row between Sayer and a female colleague with whom he has, presumably, just spent the night. The girl attacks him for his heartlessness – 'you're inhuman [...] One of the girls [in the office] told me that every time she sees a piece of cold meat hanging in a butcher's she thinks of you' (*ME* 16) – but he remains thoroughly indifferent to her outburst. His motive for agreeing to meet with Regan and write the defamatory article is also suspect, not so much due to his passionate politics but his own feelings of guilt and of being an outsider.

As a child Sayer had enjoyed a secure and comfortable middle-class existence in England which he guiltily recalls at various points in the novel, and his antipathy for the bourgeoisie seems a form of displaced self-loathing for his origins in this 'elsewhere' of social advantage. In addition, his ideological disdain for the bourgeoisie seems but a small part of a general hostility to humanity regardless of class. In a similar way to Regan he is 'without a soul' – 'I have no family' (*ME* 24) he declares to Gerhardt – and he considers emotional encounters as retarding and obscuring his impersonal function as 'the emissary of the Party, a passive instrument which it used as it saw fit for the good of the oppressed' (*ME* 178). For Sayer, the 'new man' of the revolution 'would be different. He would be hard and ruthless. There would be no compromises, no monuments to sentimentality. If a man weakened, as Regan had weakened, he would be destroyed' (*ME* 33).

Yet it is sentiment and affect which Sayer encounters and struggles with at Regan's comfortable house. At first Sayer's sojourn oddly revivifies him as the house connects him with a range of feelings which ordinarily he would dismiss as 'sentimental'. At one point he reflects upon the curious beauty of the banister next to the stairs which he finds oddly pleasing: 'he had experienced the same sensation before once or twice, when looking, for example, at the shadows thrown on the pavement by railings in the sun...or...what?' (*ME* 56). Later he is discovered on the grass outside the house in a moment of silent reverie by Gretchen, to whom he confesses that he was dreaming of being young again: 'It was only a feeling, really...Yes, a feeling that I was a schoolboy again and that it was the first day of the summer holidays and a limitless number of sunny, carefree days were stretching ahead a...wonderful feeling' (*ME* 127). His stay has perhaps reawakened submerged memories of that comfortable childhood elsewhere.

His emotions are also stimulated by Gretchen herself, and a mutual attraction grows between them. Sayer eventually rejects the possibility of a love relationship with her, choosing to place his ideological beliefs before his sentiments. Yet his feelings for Gretchen compromise his final confrontation with Regan. On the one hand, Sayer attacks Regan as part of the former's role as the mouthpiece of the Party; but also, and on the other hand, Sayer's challenge is driven by his sentiments regarding the mistreatment of Gretchen and Regan's wife. Realizing that he is getting sucked into the very world of sentiment and privilege that he has committed his life to overthrowing, Sayer decides to quit the house immediately after his major confrontation with Regan. A man weakened by sentiment, we recall, in Sayer's view deserved to be destroyed. Significantly, just before he leaves Sayer leans over the sleeping figure of Gretchen and says 'softly and bitterly: "You've destroyed me...you and Regan between you. I hope it makes you happy"' (*ME* 185). There are no victors at the end of this ugly affair.

If Sayer begins the novel indifferent to sentimentality, by the end he has not gained emotional fulfilment but recognized its absence in his own life. Indifference has been replaced with remorse. Like Regan, he is painfully exposed to his lack of 'soul', and there is no redemption or happiness for him at the novel's end. The final chapter is set in Paris and concerns a meeting between Gretchen and Sayer. The possibility of a union between the characters is mooted but quickly withdrawn. Sayer's heart sinks when he realises that Gretchen is going away to travel. He has given up his job at the newspaper 'to think things out' (*ME* 187). He has lost some of his ideological certainty and is increasingly sensitive to emotion and affect, yet he seems more miserable as a consequence with new regrets added to his long-term woes. He too ends the novel 'without a soul', alone in the world. He realizes that the love he thought he shared with Gretchen is as illusory and synthetic as the Medici fountain they walk past and contemplate before parting.

The bleakness of the world depicted in *A Man From Elsewhere* lies in the fact that the wonderful feelings, like those Sayer experienced on the grass at Regan's house, are not annihilated. Instead they seem forever 'elsewhere', suspended in another time or another place, locked away in dreams or memories, available only in the head rather than in the world. This is a novel about the absence of souls, not their inexistence. Each character searches for fulfilment and freedom despite the novel's blunt depiction of the world as a soul-less place. This point is forcefully made by the references to the horrors of German fascism, violent conflicts in contemporary Berlin and Algeria, and the impending threat of nuclear war which is discussed at one point in the text (*ME* 57). In the novel's occasional sub-plot, Luc the scriptwriter attempts to attain his own freedom by quitting his work, leaving his long-time partner Mado and setting out on a solitary quest for fulfilment. The result is a series of banal adventures. His heroic attempt to assist an Algerian being racially abused makes him the subject of mockery, and he allows himself to be seduced by the daughter of a hotelier, Monique, much to his self-disgust: 'This was not what he had come for. He had come to purify himself and not to yield himself up to adolescent girls' (*ME* 167). At the end of the novel we learn that he has returned to Mado and has plans to marry her, yet their relationship seemed to epitomize Luc's misery throughout the novel.

This failed journey undercuts the hope of Gretchen's freedom, which we learn about at the end of the text. She has dreamed that 'one day she would be free and would answer to nobody' (*ME* 59). Regan's death has made her travels possible, yet in rejecting Sayer's belated offer of union in favour of her own isolated wanderings she perhaps replicates the arrogance and remoteness of both Regan's philosophy and Sayer's earlier hard-heartedness. For Regan, Sayer and Luc, Gretchen functioned as a symbolic 'soul'. Her relationship with Regan underlines his heartlessness. She exposes Sayer to affection and sentiment while Luc's affair with her compensates for his frustrations concerning his unhappy long-term relationship with Mado, and his repeated production of cliché film scripts. Significantly then, at the end of the novel Gretchen slips away to a nameless 'elsewhere' carrying with her the possibility of an alternative life of the soul which Sayer momentarily glimpsed in Saint Guilhelm.

Farrell famously distanced himself from *A Man From Elsewhere* in later life, commenting that he wanted to buy all those copies in circulation and pulp them.[3] Critics have also taken a dim view of the text, seeing it as a minor work of curiosity or, less generously, a failure. It is a much better book than is generally assumed, but its shortcomings appear particularly visible when placed in relation to Farrell's subsequent work, especially its mercilessly gloomy atmosphere and stubborn refusal of redemption or relief. It is, as a novel, without a soul. Like the Empire Trilogy it is characterised by a steady feeling of decline and decay, in this instance derived from the demise of Regan whose descent towards death structures the rhythm and sets the overall tone of the narrative. The later novels offset this melancholic mood ('One day we shall vanish') against comic modes of writing and a tightly-controlled and ironic sentimentalism ('how lovely we are!') with remarkable results. However, in *A Man From Elsewhere* the bleak, dispiriting atmosphere extinguishes the possibility of nuance and shade.

In Farrell's next novel, *The Lung* (1965), a more respiratory environment is created, although the tone remains dark. It evidences the emergence of the particularly dissonant tone of Farrell's writing – juxtaposing melancholy with wit – that would become the major characteristic of his mature style. Ralph Crane and Jennifer Livett have compared Farrell's early novels to Samuel Beckett's prose, especially the Beckett of the 'Trilogy': *Molloy* (1950), *Malone Meurt* (1951) and *L'Innomable* (1952). They suggest that Farrell was influenced by the absurd predicament of human existence captured in Beckett's famous phrase 'I can't go on, I'll go on'.[4] If *A Man From Elsewhere* is rather too preoccupied with the first part of this quotation, *The Lung* moves the focus more to the implications of the second part. Like its predecessor, it is very much a gloomy contemplation of the pointlessness and unhappiness of human life. But it is also a book which tentatively explores survival, perseverance, recuperation and the will to live in a futile world.

The Lung is the finest of the early novels. Spanning a twelve-month period, the narrative begins and ends at Easter, suggesting themes of death and resurrection, endings and endurance, pain and panacea. Drawing upon Farrell's own experiences of suffering and surviving polio, much of the novel is set in a hospital and includes several characters whose emotional or physical ailments are in danger of proving terminal. Its hero, the journalist Martin Sands, is at first sight another glum, melancholy individual who, as his name implies, suffers from emotional and existential aridity. The novel opens with the uneasy and ironic reunion of Sands with his ex-wife Sally and her new partner Louis at a mutual friend's wedding. Also present are Sally's daughter, Marigold, and her companion Dr Baker. At the wedding reception Sands's eccentric and increasingly drunken behaviour is the source of much concern. Eventually he is rushed to the hospital where Marigold and Dr Baker work and is diagnosed as suffering from polio. Unable to breathe or move freely, he is placed in an iron lung which, although assisting with his breathing, renders him physically immobile. His upper body is irreparably damaged by polio and he never regains full use of his arms. The novel depicts Sands's gradual and partial physical recovery as he slowly regains a degree of mobility. It invites us to consider if (as with Sayer) his dismal view of the pointlessness of life has significantly altered by the novel's close when he leaves for London 'to get some things straightened out' (*L* 172).

Sands's depressive attitudes are linked to two related incidents. While working as a journalist he had been asked to interview the parents of a young girl killed in a plane crash. The incident exposed his unhappy complicity in the business of newspapers feeding off the tragedies of others, while suggesting both life and love as unhappy delusions, temporary refuges from the cruelty, inescapability and arbitrariness of death. Such were Sands's reflections when climbing the stairs to his apartment after the interview:

> All who love are blind. That was a line from yet another song. And who could deny the evidence of it as he looked at those two shattered people politely going through the motions of being reasonable and alive when they were already deader than their daughter. I'll never work as a reporter again, never, he had promised on those furious stairs. And, curiously enough, he never had. (*L* 72)

Life seems nothing but a useless cycle of 'going through the motions'. As symbolized by the couple's dead daughter, all the hope and promise of youth exists only to be vanquished. To make matters worse, on reaching the top of the stairs and entering his apartment Sands discovered his wife Sally in bed with their lodger Louis. The incident clinched his sense of disgust with life and he left the country for Canada to recuperate after the revelation of his wife's affair.

Sands's sojourn in the iron lung calls his existential bluff. Gloomy sentiments of human futility and the pointlessness of life are perhaps easy to afford if we are in perfect health, but something else entirely when illness brings us to death's door. The lung literalizes Sands's musings on the emptiness of existence by imprisoning him in inertia, immobilizing him in a contraption in which 'he was merely a part of the machinery' (*L* 56) and where he feels 'as horizontal and as petrified as a stone crusader' (*L* 56). He loses responsibility for his very body; he is respirated by the lung, washed and massaged by the hospital staff and fed through a tube. Those passages describing Sands's hellish time cocooned in the lung – with only the ceiling to look at, unable to move to relieve the acute discomfort of lying too long in one position, abandoned to his incessantly bleak thoughts – are some of the most powerful in Farrell's work and no doubt recall his own unhappy days in an iron lung. Much of Sands's discomfort in the lung stems from mental rather than physical pain. He becomes little more than his consciousness and is soon tortured by the 'terrifying world of fantasy' (*L* 71) into which he descends at night.

Yet as a consequence of Sands's despairing, unbearable illness there is also an important discovery, the faintest shadow of 'the will to live [which] stirred and fluttered its wings feebly like a freezing bird' (*L* 44). Later in the novel Sands is shocked by the sight in a mirror of his emaciated and crippled body: 'Every bone stood out clearly and between the higher ribs he could see a regular, tremulous flutter from the beating of his heart, while the lower ribs expanded like opening fingers with each breath he took' (*L* 116). *The Lung* juxtaposes the relentless, deathly juggernaut of Sands's disenchantment and anguish with the small, tremulous flutter or flicker of this 'will'. Like Sands's immobile existence in the lung which symbolises both captivity and determination, these vital signs of endurance – of the will to 'go on' – are never totally frozen. It is a point very much emphasized by the symbolic landscape of the novel. On several occasions the grounds which surround the hospital are described as distinctly wintry and freezing. Yet as Sands improves the seasons turn from autumn to winter and ultimately spring, emphasizing growth and creation. In this spirit we might read the hospital as a metaphorical iron lung through which the pulse of a will to live survives, albeit dimly, in an icy, snowbound world.

Sands's tentative progress, both physical and emotional, owes much to his relationships with two important groups at the hospital: the male patients residing in the ward to which he is eventually moved after he regains some ability to breathe unassisted; and the young women he encounters, specifically Marigold (his stepdaughter) and Monica, a fifteen-year-old patient. His fellow male patients consist of Exmoore, a preacher who lost his faith while delivering a sermon; Harris, a once-famous cricketer haunted by the senselessness of the sport and his success; and Wilson, the most mysterious of the three, who is obsessed with road traffic accidents and spends one evening in the nearby village puncturing car tyres in an attempt to reduce such fatalities. A motley crew of lively and bizarre personalities, each has suffered a traumatic experience and is individually prone to attacks of melancholy and rage.

Collectively they make an absurd but entertaining group and their behaviour elicits much humour in the novel. They often bicker and argue, yet there is a compelling sense of camaraderie which comes to act as an important support network. Sands spends time with Exmoore and especially Harris talking about their problems while confronting some of his own, underlining the possible therapeutic effects of their time together. But this recovery room remains a fragile space. Wilson's tyre-slashing episode prompts a visit to the ward from the local police inspector whom Exmoore, Harris and Sands intimidate in an attempt to protect Wilson from the law (only the intervention of a doctor diverts a potentially nasty scene). Later that night Wilson thanks the group before secretly taking some sleeping pills. He is dead the next morning.

Sands's limited recovery is also supported by his encounters with Marigold and Monica, which bring into focus the important issue of youth in *The Lung*. It gradually surfaces that he has spent much of the forty-four years of his life seducing women (one encounter occurred only weeks after he married Sally): 'Seducing women is the only thing I ever really seem to have done of any significance, I suppose. It's the only way I used to know I was alive' (*L* 101). Early in the novel we learn that Sands regards his stepdaughter as extremely sexually attractive. Throughout his stay at the hospital he embarks on the comic conquest of Marigold's virginity, a situation which brings him into conflict with the similarly amorous Exmoore. He achieves his goal one evening in a bizarre scene at the remedial swimming pool in which he has been exercising his damaged body. But rather than bring feelings of satisfaction and illusions of grandeur, the next morning Sands feels disgusted with himself: 'In order to prove his superiority over Exmoore he had won something he did not want. This was the very mediocrity he used to sneer at in other people' (*L* 153).

Throughout the novel youth has been represented as the prized possession which is too quickly lost in an ultimately miserable world, and the end of youth lies behind much of the novel's melancholy. Youth is connected to vitality, possibility and promise. Each of the male patients have, in their different ways, lost their youthful selves. Harris the cricketer's trauma has much to do with ageing. He remarks that 'I had some good times when I was younger' (*L* 100) and 'Sport is fine for a young man but when you begin to get past it...' (*L* 86). Sands's illness forces him to face up to the fact that he is not the person he once was, a realization which he had repressed for many years prior to his illness. In one telling moment, Harris throws an orange to Sands which he tries and fails instinctively to catch because of his damaged arms. In apologizing for his forgetfulness, Harris remarks 'I suppose one gets used to it after a while. It's almost as if one has become a different person all of a sudden' (*L* 122).

At one level, *The Lung* is a kind of 'anthem for a doomed youth' with Sands's illness as the metaphor for the inevitable decay of youthful vitality. His disgust at his conquest of Marigold stems from his realization that he has been complicit in the beginning of the end of her youthful innocence and hope: 'She's just a child, he thought. What on earth am I doing?' (*L* 131). This glimmer of conscience distances him from his characteristic 'collossal indifference' (*L* 92) to others. Sands's encounter with Marigold makes him reflect critically, and with some shame, upon his life as a serial seducer and his marriage to Sally: 'That's what I lost, he thought, because I was too shy and self-conscious. My youth. [...] and it was stupid to spend so much of my life trying to get it back' (*L* 166).

Sands's relationship with Monica is also vital to the theme of youth and the process of Sands's recovery, however slight this might prove to be. Ironically, Monica believes Sands to be dead when she is first wheeled past his bed in a hospital corridor (he has pulled the sheet over his head) and is pleased to revive him by engaging him in conversation. Immediately after their first encounter Sands thinks that 'It was high time he got out of the bloody place and started living again' (*L* 111). He makes her a gift of a small golden crucifix borrowed from Exmoore, invoking themes of resurrection and renewal. When Sands had first arrived at the hospital he noticed a wooden sign cut in the shape of a pointing hand which was ominously 'pointing down into the lawn itself' (*L* 38), as a reminder perhaps of the ultimate terminus for every human journey. In a symbolic reversal late in the novel, Sands and Monica walk past the wooden sign which Sands adjusts to point to the sky for a bit of 'fun' (*L* 156). Monica epitomizes the hopes of youth and appears in the novel most frequently in the spring months. She is ebullient and excited by the world. She takes Sands on walks around the hospital's wintry grounds searching out rabbits and fertile streams. But like the girl in the air crash (and Angela Spencer in *Troubles*) she is also a doomed youth. Before leaving the hospital Sands learns that she has leukaemia:

> He was silent, thinking of Monica's slender neck bent forward as he had fastened the clasp around it, bent forward to receive the blow of the axe. He thought of her growing up for nothing. Her body developing into a woman's body for nothing. All her desires and dreams and personality conceived for nothing. Monica! It was impossible to think of her dying. (*L* 172)

The news of Monica's illness is given by Dr Baker who adds that, given Sands's nihilistic attitude to life, he doubts if this news will mean very much. Sands's retort – 'It does, as it happens. But it doesn't do a damn bit of good' (*L* 172) – is less important than the doctor's reply: 'Perhaps not to her' (*L* 172). Like Sands, *The Lung* never tries to escape the cold fact of mortality and the inevitable, unstoppable approach of death. Yet at its conclusion Sands is no longer paralyzed by this fact into indifference but possesses a degree of animation in which we detect again the faint pulse of survival, for himself and for others. This is perhaps the 'good' which Dr Baker identifies and which makes Monica's approaching death something other than proof of the cruelty and absurdity of existence. It may be our fate to perish, but human life matters; it may have a meaning that survives the fact of our death. This is by no means an optimistic or even redemptive conclusion. However in this tremulous flutter of Sands's emotions we witness the beginning of the end of his 'collossal indifference' to life (*L* 92) which, hitherto, has led him into a series of meaningless, vacant sexual encounters that shore up his contempt of others. It is the first step in an attempt to 'go on'. As Dr Baker reminds him, 'You've been sick. Don't ask too much of yourself. It takes time learning to live again' (*L* 173).

The Lung was undoubtedly Farrell's attempt to think through the experiences and changes wrought by his own illness. Within a matter of months he had been prematurely transformed from a muscular, athletic twenty-one year old into a white-haired casualty of a potentially terminal condition. *The Lung* is a testimony to Farrell's dramatic and unexpected loss of youth, and the intense pain – physical and mental – it brought. Yet it also suggests something of his own resilience and fortitude. Although the novel portrays crippling illness, mental trauma, suicide, doomed youth, broken virginity and failed marriages, it is also, and importantly, an extremely funny novel. In a crucial departure from *A Man From Elsewhere*, the narrative of *The Lung* tends frequently towards black comedy. Often this is a consequence of Farrell's choice of simile or metaphor which makes the most bizarre yet oddly appropriate juxtapositions. Often, although not exclusively, this involves representing characters almost as animals: in *Troubles*, and as we shall see, Edward Spencer is distinctly leonine; in *The Siege of Krishnapur* the Collector appears almost like an overgrown cat. The effect can be both comic and grotesque, endearing yet bizarre. To take an example from *The Lung*, here is the description of Sands struggling to put on his overcoat with his immobilized arms:

> In theory he knew how to put his overcoat on. But in practice he never succeeded. First, one puts the damaged arm into its sleeve. Second, one whisks the coat round to land on the other shoulder. Third, one contorts one's good arm into the other sleeve. He whisked ineffectually for a while and then collapsed on his bed in hysterics. Harris and Exmoore watched him for a moment, launched themselves smoothly from their beds like alligators taking to the water, and set to work on him. (*L* 154)

At an immediate level the image of 'alligators taking to the water' brilliantly captures the swift and silent movement of Exmoore and Harris as they come to Sands's aid. More significantly, its unexpectedness and incongruity interrupt and lighten an otherwise sober account of a highly unsettling incident. Like Sands, the novel as a whole is saved by such moments from going into its own hysterics about illness, pain and death. These moments collectively offer a much-needed respiratory rejoinder to the suffocatingly bleak conditions it otherwise charts. *The Lung* is full of such unexpected figurative transformations: 'He folded himself carefully to the ground like a camel...' (*L* 146); '[The doctor] was standing with his arm playfully round the neck of the white metal box in the attitude of a man posing with a tiger he has recently dispatched. The lung looked at Sands and Sands looked at the lung' (*L* 53). The effect is to engender a subtle yet stubborn and wry retort to much of the solemnity and awfulness of the situations being described.

Farrell's eye for the incongruous and bizarre image would become the stylistic signature of the Empire Trilogy, but such images are about much more than simply lightening the tone of his work. Farrell's style represents his own 'tremulous flutter' of vitality as an important aesthetic principle, his particular response to the predicament of having to 'go on' in a cruel world, decanted into the act of writing. The laughter created at such moments of delightful incongruity is not a convenient escape from a world perceived as essentially cruel, but one way of enduring it. In fusing melancholy with mirth Farrell produces particular kinds of laughter that range from the hilarious to a more gentle, tender comedy. Although his novels form a diverse and variable body of work, this wonderful characteristic – for which the name 'Farrellian' is the only adequate term – rebounds throughout each of the subsequent books in varying degrees.

Laughter is in depressingly short supply in Farrell's third novel, *A Girl in the Head* (1967), which is saturated with images which emphasize gloomy endings: dying flowers, falling leaves, fading summers, failed affairs. Its tone is set by the opening paragraph with its emphasis on collapse: 'At the beginning of August a band in scarlet uniforms began to play in the municipal gardens. To Boris, watching them through binoculars from the top of a tree, they appeared like bloodstained weevils that were shortly to bring about the collapse of summer' (*GH* 7). 'Count' Boris Slattery is perhaps Farrell's most disenchanted and gloomy central character, lacking either Sayer's latent idealism or Sands's miniscule yet determined will to endure in the midst of pain and death.

Boris had stopped off in the English seaside resort of Maidenhair quite by chance while changing trains and, for no apparent reason, decided to stay. Soon after his arrival he unexpectedly saved an old woman, Granny Marie-Thé, from a certain road accident. The incident prompted an encounter between Boris and Marie-Thé's family at their Victorian home, Boscobel, where Boris met Flower, her brother Maurice (a painter) and their elderly parents, referred to throughout as Old Dongeon and Granny Dongeon. Presenting himself as a member of the aristocracy with Polish connections, 'Count' Boris wooed the Dongeons with his (probably fraudulent) display of continental sophistication and soon became a permanent fixture at Boscobel through his marriage to Flower. Much of the action in *A Girl in the Head* occurs a couple of years after their marriage during the months of August and September, the tail-end of the holiday season, and a few weeks after Boris suffered a heart attack. Also lodging at Boscobel is Alessandro, a striking Italian youth who is staying for the summer while studying in preparation for the new school he will join in September. As the novel opens, the household is awaiting the arrival from Sweden of a young girl called Inez – pronounced '*i'neige* ...like the French for "it is snowing"' (*GH* 19) – before the last days of summer dwindle into autumn.

The novel's plot deliberately lacks coherence and momentum. In terms of structure and style it is Farrell's most unconventional novel in its mixing of different narrative voices and forms. As regards the novel's 'present', the late summer days, we chiefly follow Boris on a variety of weary, often drunken visits to the pub, the cinema and the circus, as well as his working life as a waiter at a local restaurant, The Groaning Board. This narrative is interrupted by Boris's first-person account of his life history which often returns broodingly to the brief love affair he had with Ylva. There is also a third narrative voice, Boris's interior monologue. This appears twice as peculiar streams-of-consciousness set on the page as columns of increasing and decreasing thickness. The lack of chapter headings or numbers adds to the sense of arbitrariness which pervades the novel as a whole. Unlike *A Man From Elsewhere* or *The Lung*, in which a sense of momentum is established by Regan's terminal decline or Sands's partial recuperation respectively, *A Girl in the Head* lacks impetus and for the most part wanders (like Boris) aimlessly between incidents.

A measure of dynamism is eventually created when Inez arrives in September, and the developing relationship between

Inez and Alessandro (with whom she shares a room) propels the narrative in its later stages. The novel's most dramatic moment comes when Alessandro, an enthusiast of horses, and Inez go riding on the beach at Maidenhair during a thunderstorm. The weather causes Inez's horse to bolt and Alessandro sets off in pursuit with Boris absurdly joining the chase on a rusty old bicycle. Inez arrives back at Boscobel but Alessandro disappears, prompting much concern, only to be rescued by a local group of boy scouts and delivered back to Boscobel in a moment of remarkable bathos. Not long afterwards Inez and later Alessandro leave Maidenhair as the new school year beckons, and the novel concludes with Boris musing upon the fact that 'life is really rather sad when you come to think of it' (*GH* 220).

Michael C. Prusse has suggested that *A Girl in the Head* might be read as a modernist novel in the light of its narrative trickery and challenge.[5] Certainly one of the most 'modernist' aspects of the novel concerns the creation of novelistic coherence at the level of symbolic patterning rather than in terms of conventional narrative form. Much of its landscape, and virtually all of its characters, have a symbolic function which relates to a wider figurative schema. As in *The Lung*, the theme of lost or doomed youth looms large in *A Girl in the Head*, and much of the novel's symbolic superstructure can be interpreted accordingly. As a holiday resort Maidenhair is presented as an important flight from reality, an enclave from the cruel, unhappy world beyond its horizon. Boris occasionally muses on Maidenhair in these terms, noting that 'while he was standing in the nauseating unreality of Maidenhair Bay, people all over the world were dying grotesque deaths in unromantic wars' (*GH* 32). The promise of Maidenhair is frequently asserted. At one point Boris notices a line of cars inching their way into the town: 'Yes, they seemed to say, yes, even one day in a year, makes all the difference. In a lifetime, if you like. Go there just once and everything is changed' (*GH* 40).

Boris's past has been one of loss – of his lover Ylva and his mother who abandoned him very early in his life (*GH* 41) – and these representations of Maidenhair might well explain why Boris stopped there in the first place. Significantly, during his first days in the town he lodged in a greenhouse and ate only baby food (*GH* 65). This latter detail suggests that Maidenhair might be considered as a womb-like space which facilitates the return to a better, happier, younger world of innocence and security, but ultimately fails to deliver this promise. Its very name conjures both these possibilities. By punning on 'maidenhood' it gestures – via a problematic mode of representing women, to which I'll return – to an Edenic, innocent time before sexual experience. Yet 'Maiden[-]hair' also suggests a process of maturation and bodily change (it is worth noting in passing that 'maiden hair' also prompts a certain moment of maturation for two naive young men, Harry and Fleury, in *The Siege of Krishnapur*). Boris's stay in Maidenhair is his attempt to escape back to that younger, idyllic world, yet his experience of Maidenhair only serves to bring him face-to-face with the inevitable process of maturation.

Boris's initial sojourn in a greenhouse calls attention to the importance of images of plantlife in the novel and asks us to consider human life as nothing more than a kind of vegetation. Maidenhair is 'like a giant plant that flowered and withered according to a natural cycle' (*GH* 90). We first spy Boris at the beginning of the novel sitting at the top of the sycamore tree which stands outside his bedroom window, scanning the horizon through a pair of binoculars (comically he has to be rescued from the tree by the fire brigade). It is a moment which anticipates a scene later in the novel when Boris, ever the voyeur, has drilled a hole in the floor of his room and spies upon Alessandro and Inez in the room below. The positioning of Boris 'above' also occurs during a party:

> [Boris] was isolated. He was looking down on the room from above. He saw the criss-cross threads of emotion with which, like mountaineers, the people in the room were trying to rope themselves together for the slow, dangerous ascent of their lives. The descent, I mean, from youth and strength. The descent from dreams. I know all about that, he thought, pulling with unsteady fingers at a loose thread of black cotton that hung irritatingly from the crutch of his blue jeans. (*GH* 157)

This descent 'from youth and dreams' is symbolized by the steady decline of Maidenhair's plantlife as summer turns to autumn (there is no springtime in this novel, in contrast to *The Lung*). Boris represents this as 'a cycle of impersonal change' in which human beings are caught up 'like vegetables' (*GH* 167).

He comes to regard the natural world as living proof of the pointless cycles of generation and degeneration which make life little more than a brief flowering of youth followed by the inevitable deathly descent. The novel is full of references to dying or declining flowers. In the opening chapter Boris encounters a 'dazzling sunflower' which disconcerts him: 'As he knelt there [looking at the sunflower] he was suddenly appalled by its fragility. Death, he thought. Death before winter' (*GH* 10). The sunflower proves that 'the seasons are remorseless. There's no difference between being magnificently golden and lifelessly withered. The circle chases itself eternally' (*GH* 84). Near the end of the novel Boris is suspected of smashing a potted yellow chrysanthemum given by Inez to Flower as a gift. And, of course, there is Flower herself, whose relationship with Boris seems to epitomize decline. Flower has suffered a miscarriage, and her marriage with Boris seems arid and unfulfilling (Boris moves into a room of his own during the novel). It has failed 'to bloom satisfactorily' (*GH* 146). Boris significantly uses nature imagery to represent their marriage as a disappointment: 'I was like a man who sees a breeze playing over a field of corn and is so inspired by its beauty that he buys it. Well, I bought the field but I couldn't buy the breeze. The breeze dropped' (*GH* 146).

In a way which recalls the figure of Monica in *The Lung*, Alessandro and Inez represent the verve and possibilities of youthful lives that are teetering precariously on the brink of adulthood and experience. Alessandro's passion for riding horses embodies much of this youthful energy, and we glimpse him frequently in the novel riding across the dunes of Maidenhair's beach sporting a vivid red cape which contrasts starkly with the grey surroundings of the bay. It is as if Boris sees in Alessandro an image of his dashing lost younger self, a connection we are invited to make when we learn that Alessandro's cape has been borrowed from Boris. In a similar fashion, Inez is represented as a figure of purity and perfection. Her name, recalling the French term for snow, supplements her symbolic importance as a vision of purity and undefiled perfection. In one incident Boris watches her bathing naked in the sea from whence she emerges looking like Bottecelli's *The Birth of Venus*:

Inez was now standing naked and motionless at the water's edge, with a serene half-smile on her lips as if at the recollection of some pleasant memory. Her slender right hand was raised to cover her breasts while the other trailed down absently over her sex. Her hair flowed down over her shoulders in golden waves. And there she stood, motionless, beside the sea. [...] Boris groaned. He had never seen a girl of such beauty. (*GH* 116)

This aestheticizing vision of Inez specifically tries to hide the presence of her physical maturation, denying her burgeoning womanhood by constructing her specifically as a 'girl'. The hand which trails 'absently' over 'her sex' and 'maiden-hair' indexes this attempt to absent any adult sexual identity from Inez. She is, for Boris, simply 'perfect' (*GH* 144): a 'girl in the head', a symbol of idyllic, idealized youth, yet who will encounter adulteration in a corrupt world. Much of Boris's concern about her sharing of a room with Alessandro (and his peculiar desire to spy on their nocturnal activities) springs from a need to place Inez beyond the possibility of sexual experience, of 'deflowering'. Together, these characters come to represent everything which Boris feels he has lost and which requires protection from the cruel realities of the adult world. It is a situation epitomized by one of Maurice's paintings significantly called 'A Maiden's Honour' which hangs in the dining room at Boscobel. The painting depicts an old man presenting a purse of gold coins to 'a concupiscent old lady with heavily rouged cheeks', whose daughter 'had snatched up the carving-knife and was about to plunge it into her already somewhat dishevelled bodice' (*GH* 17). First love creates the necessity for last rites; the transition from youth into adulthood is a kind of death.

The scene where Alessandro and Inez disappear on horseback during the storm, pursued by Boris, is of particular symbolic importance. Boris follows their trail into a strange wood – itself a dark, dangerous, liminal space associated with the cruel world of experience – on a rickety bicycle which contrasts with the muscular horses ridden by the 'children'. This emphasizes Boris's declining position on the 'cycle' of existence. In a peculiar moment of reverie he imagines that 'somewhere in the distance ahead those two superb horses were sailing effortlessly over a sunlit meadow, their riders laughing with the gaiety of their indescribable youth, hair streaming on the warm summer breeze' (*GH* 180). Immediately he falls off his bicycle and lies semi-conscious on the ground, where 'a large, dead sycamore leaf' lands on his face despite their being 'no sycamore tree in sight' (*GH* 181). This detail returns us to the sycamore tree outside Boscobel in which we first spied Boris. It suggests that the tree epitomizes the maturity and process of ageing from which he will never be rescued despite his attempt (and the holidaymakers in Maidenhair) to escape this reality or protect those whose youth is, like the summer, almost over.

In the final chapter of the novel we learn that Boris has chopped down the tree to leave only a stump, signifying both his outrage at this immovable fact of his existence and his impotent attempts to resist it. Indeed, Boris's action has been prompted by a startling discovery in the final pages of the novel of Inez and Maurice copulating in the dunes. This moment signals the victory of the world of experience over that idealized realm of innocence and purity. It also suggests that the woman in the dunes has not been the idyllic 'girl in the head', that is, the Inez of Boris's imagination.

Boris suffers from a degree of idealism and is ripe for a fall, and in this regard he anticipates several of Farrell's characters in the Empire Trilogy, such as the Oxford undergraduates in *Troubles*, Fleury in *The Siege of Krishnapur* and Matthew Webb in *The Singapore Grip*. But his relentless, depressing view of life is also extremely tiresome and causes exasperation for others in the novel, if not the reader. One of his friends, Dr Cohen, takes him to a hospital gymnasium where a variety of young patients are trying to exercise their fragile, crippled bodies. Despite upsetting Boris, Dr Cohen claims that he is trying to help him: 'You probably have another twenty or thirty years to serve on this planet. I'm just trying to make it easier for you' (*GH* 89).

Doctors appear frequently in Farrell's fiction: Dr Baker in *The Lung*, Dr Ryan in *Troubles* and Dr McNab in both *The Siege of Krishnapur* and *The Hill Station*. They often represent a pragmatic outlook on life, resigned to yet not traumatised by mortality, which offsets the kind of gloominess which Boris prefers. The gymnasium recalls the space and predicament in which Sands found himself in *The Lung*, and where a flutter of the will to survive might also be discovered. But Boris, peering in from the outside, sees only 'cripples' (*GH* 89). Significantly, Dr Cohen dies later in the novel and any resigned pragmatism dies with him. Boris's pessimistic outlook is thus never sufficiently displaced and is allowed to stand relatively unchallenged. The predominant symbol of the novel is ultimately provided by the circus (the name of which also evokes notions of circularity and repetition) which comes to Maidenhair. Boris notices a poster advertising the circus which features Lady Jane, a lion tamer whose act involves her putting her head into a lion's mouth. This alternative image of 'a girl in the head' wins out in the end against the idealized vision of Inez and signals her unavoidable fate, soon to be ravished by the 'naked jaws' (*GH* 32) of a corrupting world.

Boris's attraction to the poster of Lady Jane also has a sexual dimension, stimulated by the image of her 'clad in white trousers and shirt tapping her black boots with an enormous whip. Beside her a lion sat on a stool and gazed with interest at her bulging breasts' (*GH* 28). This is one of several pictures in the novel which tend to depict women with recourse to a depressingly familiar dichotomy as either asexual innocents or seductresses – Inez or Lady Jane. Indeed, hanging opposite the painting of 'A Maiden's Honour' in the dining room at Boscobel is another of Maurice's paintings, 'The Rewards of Luxury', which depicts the biblical scene of Salome with John the Baptist's head.

One incident in the novel concerns an uncomfortable sexual encounter between Boris and June, a young local girl, which occurs in a boat-house. Boris is forced to pay the boatman, who is minding the boathouse for his boss, in order for the couple to gain access. Their intercourse is brief and unrewarding – Boris is disappointed by the 'hardness' of her body and the appearance of her pubic hair 'like a wad of steel wool' (*GH* 95). The absurdity of the scene is accentuated by June accidentally sitting upon a recently-varnished boat which leaves two sticky patches on her buttocks. The incident is important in revealing that Boris is perhaps little different to his brother-in-law Maurice. Both are complicit in the corruption of young girls, and hence Boris's care for the purity and perfection of youth is compromised by his own 'mature' sexual urges which ultimately make him into a hypocrite.

A Girl in the Head is locked too securely inside Boris's dismal consciousness, with laughter less forthcoming than in *The Lung* and it also perpetuates more than it ironizes the problematic representation of women as either angels or whores. There is very little else to Inez, Flower, Lady Jane and June beyond the male characters' use and depiction of them, and the novel as a whole seems to lack interest in female characters as anything other than symbols. This is an accusation which might be raised at the portrayal of women in each of Farrell's early novels when we recall Gretchen's role as the symbolic absent soul of *A Man From Elsewhere* or Monica's function as a symbol of doomed youth in *The Lung*. Yet the previous novels are also interested in these characters as being much more than figurative icons and they tend not to evoke the kinds of representational clichés which *A Girl in the Head* frequently reaches for. This is, I would suggest, more a result of the novel's flawed design, which fails to ironize fully Boris's problematic perceptions, than it is a comment on Farrell's view of women. Certainly the later novels reveal a more sophisticated representation of women which one would expect from an intelligent writer. None the less, this unresolved problem with the novel makes its achievement merely moderate.

Ralph Crane has defended *A Girl in the Head* as 'an excellent novel that has been seriously neglected by critics'.[6] While I would agree that it has been too frequently neglected as an important work in its own right, any excellence is tarnished by the overpowering authority of Boris's bankrupt consciousness. Ultimately, *A Girl in the Head* seems too disenchanted with life, too gloomy about the terminal condition of youth, and uncomfortably complicit with Boris's dichotomizing view of women.

Until very recently Farrell's early novels had not been given much critical attention and were regarded as minor works when set against the Empire Trilogy.[7] One example would be Ronald Binns's view that *A Man From Elsewhere* shows Farrell 'toying with techniques and themes later to become central to his historical novels'.[8] It is perhaps a little unfair to tether the early novels too securely to the Empire Trilogy which would succeed and overshadow them. In particular *The Lung* is an admirable novel that deserves attention (and reprinting) on its own merits. Several elements from the early works certainly reappear: the unflinching emphasis on decay and decline as a major theme, a sense of humour born from incongruity, a bleak view of human life, challenges to ideological and philosophical convictions. Yet if the early novels do have a lesson to teach us about how we might approach the Empire Trilogy, it is the suggestion that we attend to the important differences between them as well as their connections. *A Man From Elsewhere*, *The Lung* and *A Girl in the Head* are identifiably the work of a single writer, yet they differ from each other in significant ways that make it problematical to regard them as a coherent body of work. Thus, the early novels are best considered as three different, if related, novels and *not* as the same novel of existential gloom in three alternative guises. In turning next to the Empire Trilogy, it is wise to keep this observation fully in focus.

3
Ireland, 1919–1921

The first part of the Empire Trilogy, *Troubles,* signifies an important departure in Farrell's writing, although many of its aspects are redolent of the early fiction. Much of the novel's power derives from the encounter between the emotive issues of the 1960s novels – melancholy, the premature end of youth, illness, unrequited love, mortality and decline – and a new set of historical, political and literary concerns. *Troubles*, then, is best thought of as a transitional novel, announcing a new direction but drawing upon familiar preoccupations.

In setting *Troubles* in Ireland between July 1919 and the late Summer of 1921, Farrell turned to a period of public rather than private crisis. During these months the Irish fought a successful War of Independence against the occupying British colonial forces. The result was the signing of the Anglo-Irish Treaty of 6 December 1921, which formally relinquished British rule in Ireland and established a self-governing Irish Free State for twenty-six of its thirty-two counties. In looking to the past for inspiration, Farrell also turned to different kinds of novelistic genres – the Anglo-Irish 'Big House' novel, the colonial adventure story, the blockbuster – which he recast in terms of the ironic, melancholic and darkly comic vision that had been nurtured in the early novels.

It is important to recognize from the outset that the Empire Trilogy is written with a high level of literary self-reflexivity and playfulness which are crucial aspects of Farrell's ironic and critical representation of the British overseas. Early readers tended to consider Farrell as a conventional novelist who had chosen to eschew the vogue for novelistic experimentation in the 1960s and early 1970s in favour of conventional fictional modes. According to Neil McEwan, Farrell 'accepts the older conventions of modern prose narrative and believes they reflect what we normally experience'.[1] More recently (and, to my mind, more accurately), critics have shown that this view is maybe mistaken, and have suggested that the Empire Trilogy's literary self-consciousness and generic playfulness are very similar to the characteristics of 'postmodern' fiction, especially the tendency towards parody.[2] Coupled with Farrell's continuing delight in bizarre and unexpected metaphors, which we considered in the previous chapter, his playful attitude to literary genre contributes to the increasingly complex role of humour in his novels.

Troubles concerns the visit of Major Brendan Archer, a veteran of the First World War, to the west of Ireland in the summer of 1919 to be reunited with his fiancée Angela Spencer, to whom he became rashly engaged in 1916. Angela lives in the village of Kilnalough with her father Edward and brother Ripon at the vast Majestic hotel which stands on a slim coastal peninsula. The Spencers and the Majestic reflect the predominantly Protestant and doomed Anglo-Irish Ascendancy class in Ireland, loyal to Britain and the Empire, fearful of Irish independence and Catholic rule. On arrival, the Major is disconcerted to discover that the Majestic is in a decrepit state. Inadequately staffed and falling into disrepair, its main inhabitants are the old ladies who seem to have settled there permanently, a skeleton domestic staff, Edward's dogs and prize pigs, and a swelling population of cats which haunts the upper reaches of the hotel. Angela seems happy at the Major's arrival but soon mysteriously disappears from view. Frustrated, within a few weeks the Major decides to quit Kilnalough, which is becoming increasingly dangerous as a consequence of the growing conflict between the Irish Republican Army (IRA) and the British forces. But during a visit to Dublin to watch the Peace Day parade, he learns that Angela has died from leukaemia and returns to the Majestic for the funeral.

This does not spell the end of the Major's attachment to Kilnalough. In the early weeks of his stay in Ireland he also befriends a local Irish girl, Sarah Devlin, towards whom he develops romantic feelings. On returning to London to care for his sick Aunt in the Autumn of 1919, the Major corresponds with Sarah and briefly entertains her in London. He returns to

Kilnalough in 1920 in pursuit of Sarah and lodges once more with the Spencers. Thus begins a complicated year of sojourn at the Majestic, with the Major in timid pursuit of his new love. As 1920 turns into 1921, the situation in Ireland continues to worsen and attacks on the British and Anglo-Irish increase, with bloody reprisals by the Crown's forces. Conscious of the declining prestige and power of the Anglo-Irish Ascendancy, and perplexed by the turn of events in Ireland, Edward Spencer decides to hold a grand ball in an attempt to recreate the late-nineteenth-century splendour and magnificence of the Majestic and the Anglo-Irish ruling class it hosted.

Although well attended, the ball serves only to emphasize the terminal decline of the Anglo-Irish Ascendancy. On the same night, the Major's proposal of marriage to Sarah is rebuffed, and it becomes clear that she has been having an affair with Edward. Soon after the ball, Edward shoots dead a young Irish boy prowling in the hotel's grounds and, with the political situation disintegrating, the Majestic is evacuated. However, just before the Major can leave he is knocked unconscious and buried up to his neck on the beach, to be drowned by the incoming tide. In a brilliant scene of Farrellian comedy and bathos, he is rescued by the old ladies in the nick of time. The Majestic is burned to the ground, leaving only a ruin. After recovering his strength in Kilnalough, the Major returns to England in July 1921 with the statue of Venus that used to stand in the Majestic's entrance hall and magically survived the fire.

The novel's title refers us to a number of 'troubles'. The Major's troubled romantic relationships with Angela and Sarah are framed by the political troubles in Ireland. The War of Independence is gathering momentum as the novel proceeds, although the unfolding of historical events mainly happens 'off-stage' and often seems to impinge obliquely on life at the Majestic. As Tony Gould describes, 'in *Troubles* the history is very properly kept to the periphery or suggested metaphorically through the actions and fate of ordinary – though eccentric – people'.[3] *Troubles*, then, may be a novel of history, but it deliberately troubles what one might expect in a conventional historical novel by setting up a tangential and puzzling relationship between its action and events in Ireland between 1919 and 1921.

Apart from the briefest of mentions in newspaper extracts, which appear in the narrative at intervals, leading historical figures from the period such as Lloyd George, Edmund De Valera, Michael Collins and Sir Edward Carson do not feature. We see little of the bloody conflict between the warring sides which emerges in the narrative chiefly through second-hand accounts, just as the Major hears belatedly of Edward's murder of the Irish youth (the moment of his shooting is not narrated). Although a small regiment of British troops are stationed at the Majestic, we see nothing of their reprisals against Irish military operations other than the reports in the newspapers which the Major reads.

There is one brief scene set in Dublin when the Major witnesses an assassination, but for most of the novel the bloody events of history take place at a remove and only gradually impact upon lives at the Majestic. There are also very few dates given in the novel so that it becomes difficult to establish exactly when the action is taking place. As in *A Girl in the Head* there is a purposeful degree of randomness about the unfolding of events, with unrelated incidents following each other in a seemingly arbitrary fashion. Bizarrely perhaps, at the heart of this 'historical' novel reside an assembly of old ladies, eccentric residents, capricious lovers and enigmatic servants, as well as the unusual figures of Edward and the Major – and not forgetting the Majestic's bestiary of cats, dogs and pigs.

Shortly after the novel's completion Farrell explained why he had chosen an idiosyncratic approach to writing about the past:

> It is a common misconception that when the historians have finished with an historical incident there remains nothing but a patch of feathers and a pair of feet; in fact, the most important things, for the very reason that they are trivial, are unsuitable for digestion by historians, who are only able to nourish themselves on the signing of treaties, battle strategies, the formation of Shadow Cabinets and so forth. These matters are quite alien to the life most people lead, which consists of catching colds, falling in love, or falling off bicycles. [...] One of the things I have tried to do in *Troubles* is to show people 'undergoing' history, to use an expression of Sartre's.[4]

The reference to Sartre exposes the continuing influence of French intellectual culture on Farrell's writing. It also suggests that Farrell took his models for writing his fictions of British colonial history from European rather than strictly British antecedents – his other major influence in this regard being Tolstoy. In concerning himself with showing people 'undergoing' history, Farrell attends to the ways in which the tremors of weighty events are felt at minor, mundane locations seemingly remote from the personages and corridors of power. It is a way of representing history which explores how major events impact upon the minutiae of people's lives – just as a stone dropped in a pond radiates ripples which imperceptibly disturb the grass growing at the water's edge.

Consider the Major's proposal of marriage to Angela Spencer, which occurred in Brighton in 1916: 'They had kissed behind a screen of leaves and, reaching out to steady himself, he had put his hand down firmly on a cactus, which had rendered many of his parting words insincere' (*T* 11–12). These kinds of contingent, unpredictable connections between one incident (the hand on the cactus) and another (a proposal of marriage) are at the heart of *Troubles*'s humdrum representation of history, and help service much of the novel's (and the Trilogy's) humour and bathos. The incident also exemplifies Farrell's universal rejection of a heroic conception of history in favour of a combination of the peculiar and commonplace. As he further remarked in 1978, 'The real experience [of history] is not composed of treaties being signed or pincer movements. It's smoke in your eyes or a blister on your foot.'[5] Hence his central characters tend to be primarily comic figures 'undergoing history' whose behaviour (like the Major's proposal) can at times seem distinctly eccentric and occasionally slapstick. In Farrell's eyes, the subject for the historical novelist, as opposed to the historian, is the unheroic realm of 'real experience'.

Consequently, with the effects of history registered bathetically at the level of the seemingly trivial, the product is frequently laughter. Laughter fulfils an important critical role in *Troubles* and is often at the heart of Farrell's censure of Empire. Not long after the Major's arrival in Ireland, Edward's son, Ripon, tells of an incident in which Edward visited a local pub with several of the Majestic's elderly residents in order to sing the British national anthem and show the flag to the bemused drinkers. The visit was prompted by the 'Soloheadbeg affair' (*T* 85): the shooting of two Royal Irish Constabulary officers at Soloheadbeg on the 21 January 1919 by Dan Breen, an Irish

Republican Army leader from Tipperary. This incident is often regarded by historians as marking the beginning of the Irish War of Independence. After the residents sing the first two verses of 'God Save the King', creating a bizarre spectacle, there is a moment of silence:

> Then it came [said Ripon]: a great rolling storm of applause, of laughter, of clapping and crying and cheering. The noise was positively deafening. The skin that covered that straining, bulging tension in the room had broken and the relief was divine, Major. [...] Now everyone was singing, not just a few drunken tenors at the bar. It was wonderful, the way everyone was singing together. And, not content with singing, a young fellow wearing a cap much too big for him and baggy trousers that looked as if they'd been made out of potato sacks jumped up on a stool and began to conduct ... (*T* 88, 89)

As one of the old ladies says, 'You know, I think they were making fun of us.' (*T* 89). The Irish response to Edward's performance converts its imperialist gravitas into the stuff of levity via an act of parody and repetition. The laughter that results avoids the violence of confrontation yet constitutes its own critique of Edward's bombast. Much of Farrell's analysis of Empire works precisely in this fashion, and in so doing Farrell's writing aligns itself with a subaltern response to colonialism. In depicting his characters 'undergoing history' Farrell repeatedly appropriates the language and conventions of colonial society, producing laughter both recuperative and barbed.

Troubles may be an idiosyncratic and comic novel, but its humour exists cheek-by-jowl with the more sober, morbid temperament we might recognise from the earlier novels. As a shell-shocked survivor of the First World War, the Major has been exposed to all the horrors of trench warfare and has developed a fatalistic attitude to life. His experience of the horrors of war makes him seem prematurely aged, as does the retention of his title after his discharge (the narrator never refers to him as Brendon). On more than one occasion in the novel it is clear that he is still traumatized by his experiences, which contributes to a residual pensiveness on his part which is never entirely banished: 'the war was still there. He had not yet finished with it' (*T* 80).

On returning to London after the war, the Major's aunt holds a tea-party to welcome him home, at which he is discovered sitting silently in the drawing room with 'a bitter, weary expression in his eyes' (*T* 14). On another occasion he distresses his aunt by looking oddly at a number of young ladies she has invited for tea: 'he dismayed everyone by the hungry attention with which he stared at their heads, their legs, their arms. He was thinking: "How firm and solid they look, but how easily they come away from the body!" And the tea in his cup tasted like bile' (*T* 14). Later we are treated to another kind of response to the war when Sarah visits the Major in London. Comforted by her warmth, the Major begins to talk about the atrocities in the trenches until 'the bubble of bitterness in his mind slowly dissolved and tears at last began to run down his cheeks for all his dead friends' (*T* 137). The Major's attitudes are also echoed by Kilnalough's old doctor, Dr Ryan, who is resigned to the inevitable mortality of all human life: 'people are insubstantial. They really do not ever last... They never last. A doctor should know' (*T* 155). In the figure of Dr Ryan we can perhaps detect the clearest echo of the early novels, which similarly voice such sentiments through the mouths of doctors.

Throughout *Troubles* a frivolous representation of history is held in check by an awareness of the carnage of conflict. In one incident Edward becomes involved in an argument with a group of Oxford undergraduates, staying briefly at the Majestic, concerning the alleged 'treachery' of those Irish men and women involved in the Easter rebellion of 1916. During dinner, both the Major and one of the students, a veteran of the war called Captain Roberts, are called upon to support contrasting views of how troops fighting in France greeted the news: as a justified uprising or as a gross betrayal of the Empire. The argument ends with Edward storming off in a fury, much to the amusement of the undergraduates who are also tickled by the fact that revolvers have been placed at the table and that the sugar bowl contains bullets. The incident ends with the students howling with laughter 'till their ribs ached' (*T* 413), yet the responses of the war veterans hold the narrator's attention:

> It was such healthy, goodnatured laughter that even the old ladies found themselves smiling or chuckling gently. Only Captain Roberts at one table and the Major at the other showed no sign of amusement. They sat on in silence, chin in hand, perhaps, or rubbing their eyes wearily, waiting in patient dejection for the laughter to come to an end. (*T* 413)

In many ways this moment is indicative of the novel as a whole which frequently combines darker and lighter tones. Like the undergraduates who did not experience the trenches or the Easter rebellion and can discourse about historical events with detachment, there is a degree of levity in the novel's approach to a period from the past that its author obviously did not live through. Yet, like the war veterans, *Troubles* also recognizes that history is no laughing matter. It is a solemn arena where one encounters 'the vast army of the dead' (*T* 46) who died fighting for principles that – when viewed from a different political and historical vantage – seem discredited, indefensible, even absurd. The silence of the Major and Captain Roberts points towards the carnage, suffering and waste created by historical conflicts and aligns *Troubles* with Farrell's early work and its emphasis on the futility and absurdity of existence. The undergraduates' laughter is both an antidote to and a diversion from such darker moods which remain unobtrusively present throughout the novel; while the silence of Captain Roberts and the Major is a vocal representation of the unspeakable sufferings of history.

A particular element of *Troubles*'s bittersweet levity derives from its ironic use of the 'Big House' novel, a genre deployed by several Anglo-Irish writers, the origins of which can be traced to Maria Edgeworth's *Castle Rackrent* (1800). The Majestic exists in an ironic relation to the tradition of the 'Big House' novel as it is a witty symbol of the declining fortunes of the Anglo-Irish Ascendancy. The 'Big House' was, from the eighteenth century, commonly the home of wealthy Anglo-Irish Ascendancy families, existing in stark contrast to the meagre houses of the Catholic peasantry. In *Troubles* there is a marked disparity between the vast dimensions of the Majestic and the 'few wretched stone cottages with ragged, barefoot children playing in front of them' (*T* 17) which characterize Kilnalough. Jacqueline Genet argues that the Big Houses of Ireland function as a sign of the Anglo-Irish Ascendancy class as well as the authority of Empire: 'they offer an explanation of that class, its style and manners, they set out its relation with its environment and culture, and they plot its eventual disintegration and decomposition'.[6] The Majestic's eventual razing is very much part of the topos of the Big House novel, such as Elizabeth Bowen's *The Last September* (1939), and bears witness to the fortunes of many

Big Houses during the transitional months of Irish independence.

Although the Majestic clearly belongs to the tradition of the Big House, Farrell purposefully undercuts its grandeur through a series of parodic innovations which help establish a critical perspective upon the Anglo-Irish Ascendancy. In contrast to the grand country estate, the Majestic fulfils the rather more prosaic function of a hotel, emphasizing transient lodging over permanent stay. On several occasions it seems to have degenerated into a burlesque of the Big House. Consider the description of the Major's first sight of the Majestic:

> Not far away the two massive, weatherworn gateposts of the Majestic rose out of the impenetrable foliage that lined the sea side of the road. As they passed between them (the gates themselves had vanished, leaving only the skeletons of the enormous iron hinges that had once held them) the Major took a closer look: each one was surmounted by a great stone ball on which a rain-polished stone crown was perched slightly askew, lending the gateposts a drunken, ridiculous air, like solemn men in paper hats. (*T* 18)

Like the gateposts, the Majestic stands askew from the Big House, more ridiculous than grandiose. On entering the foyer, the Major notices with alarm 'the dusty gilt cherubs, red plush sofas and grimy mirrors' as well as 'the broad staircase (from which a number of brass stair-rods had disappeared, causing the carpet to bulge dangerously in places)' (*T* 19). The Majestic's upper reaches are populated by rats and cats. On his first night the Major is sickened to find a rotting sheep's head in a small cupboard next to his bed. As his stay lengthens the Majestic literally crumbles around its guests: 'the mirrors everywhere had become more fogged and grimy than ever; the gas mantles which had until recently burned on the stairs and in the corridors had now stopped functioning, so that the ladies had to grope their way to bed with their hearts going pit-a-pat' (*T* 285).

The foliage housed in the Palm Court conservatory, where the Major meets Angela on his arrival, grows wildly out of control. Sarah and the Major spend one afternoon discovering a series of alarming bulges in a number of the Majestic's rooms which appear to be roots belonging to the tropical plants housed in the Palm Court. The tennis courts become covered with a prolific type of clover which renders playing impossible, while a 'green epidemic' of ivy covers the outside walls. The remaining guests soon become used to 'the nomadic existence of moving from room to room whenever plumbing or furniture happened to fail them' (*T* 285). Such an insalubrious and decaying building could not be further from the ostentatious pretensions of the Big House.

As a symbol of crumbling authority, the Majestic is Farrell's central device for playfully portraying the doomed Empire in Ireland through a variety of metaphors. The 'green epidemic' which covers the walls, as well as the foliage which runs rampant throughout the hotel, can of course be linked to the green of Ireland and suggests Ireland's reclamation of the ground upon which the Majestic imperiously sits. The cats and dogs allegorically suggest the conflict between Irish and British forces. Edward is a great lover of dogs and is often accompanied by his favourite, Rover, an aged and ailing creature who gradually turns blind. Rover seems a comic symbol of Britain's ill fortunes in Ireland. Edward resorts to shooting Rover in order to end the dog's suffering and wounds himself in the process. Rover is buried 'standing on his hind legs, his shattered skull only a few inches below the surface of the soil' (*T* 384), an unusual posture which anticipates the Major's burial on the beach by the IRA at the novel's climax.

The deserted Imperial Bar in the Majestic is populated by a 'colony of cats' (*T* 168) which grow rapidly in number throughout the novel and have 'dominion over the upper storeys' (*T* 327). When the Majestic is being prepared for the ball Edward and the Major shoot as many cats as they can find: 'the shrieks had been terrible, unnerving, as if it were a massacre of infants that they were about – but it had to be done, in the interests of the Majestic' (*T* 327). In one memorable scene during a game of cards, a particularly large orange cat with 'acid green eyes' (T 233) attacks the hat of Miss Stavely. The cat is killed by another resident, Mr Evans, who deals it a terrible blow to its neck – causing a wail, 'thin as a shriek of a child' (*T* 235) – and throws it against the wall. The green and orange colouring of the cat clearly suggests the colours of the Irish flag, while Mr Evans's response perhaps indicates the violence being meted out to the Irish by British forces. Although Farrell does not focus directly on the armed conflict at large in the country, 'the odour of fear and violence' (*T* 237) which characterizes Ireland at this time penetrates the Majestic. The violence raging between the British and Irish forces is displaced onto the fortunes of the cats and dogs in the novel, and suggests obliquely the fighting and fatalities of the War of Independence.

Presiding over the Majestic's gradual deterioration is Edward Spencer, Farrell's chief representative of the Anglo-Irish Ascendancy and British imperialist attitudes. Like the Majestic, Edward is a parodic figure. Farrell uses him to suggest the bloody legacy of the British colonialism in Ireland, yet at times he can seem a sympathetic character, tempered by his eccentricities. Edward Spencer's name recalls that of the sixteenth-century poet Edmund Spenser, who spent a great deal of his adult life in Ireland; first, as secretary to the Governor General of Ireland, and later as the Sheriff of Cork. Scornful of the Irish, Spenser owned a three-thousand-acre estate, Kilcolm Castle, on which he intended to settle a community of English immigrants. His dismissive attitudes concerning the Irish were expressed in his treatise *A vewe of the present state of Irelande*, written in the 1590s but not printed until 1633 due to the inflammatory nature of his remarks. Like the Majestic, Kilcolm Castle was burned in October 1598 during a rebellion, and Spenser was driven back to England.[7]

By aligning the fictional Edward Spencer with an Elizabethan personage, Farrell subtly links events in 1919-1921 with a much longer history of Anglo-Irish conflict that reaches back at least to the Elizabethan period. Farrell's fictional Spencer certainly bears the traces of the Renaissance poet's attitudes to the Irish. The Major notices several 'tattered children' (*T* 187), clearly half-starving, looking for corn in the Majestic's surrounding fields. He wonders if it would be possible to educate them to the extent that one could not tell the difference between an Irish child and the son of a gentleman. Edward's response is, sadly, typical: 'You might just as well dress up a monkey in a suit of clothes' (*T* 187). The murder of the Irish boy towards the end of the novel exemplifies Edward's attitudes throughout towards the Catholic Irish.

However, Edward is *not* simply an authoritarian, colonial bigot, such as Ronny Heaslop in E. M. Forster's *A Passage to India* (1924) or District Superintendent Merrick in Paul Scott's *The*

Jewel in the Crown (1966). At times Farrell risks a more sympathetic portrayal of Edward which considerably complicates his characterization and makes *Troubles* into something much more than an anti-colonial or anti-Ascendancy tract. There is the curious fact of his appearance. The narrator tells us that Edward's strikingly leonine and rugged features are offset by his ears that are 'remarkably flattened against his skull, the reason being [Edward's] mother's horror of ears which stuck out. [...] The rugged forehead, the heavy brows, the stony set of the jaw would have been too harsh if they had not been countered by those winsomely folded ears' (*T* 27). On several occasions in the novel Edward's unpleasant attitudes are similarly countered by quirks or eccentricities which humanize him to a degree, making him appear more comic than grotesque. On the evening of the great ball, which preoccupies much of the novel's second half, he appears wearing a suit which is too small for him:

> [T]he years revealed themselves in the horizontal strain marks where the top of his trousers surrounded his stomach, in the severe grip that the coat exerted across his shoulders from one armpit to another, encouraging his arms to hang outwards, penguin fashion. Nevertheless he was an imposing figure. Evening dress suited his craggy, leonine features by putting them in a civilised perspective. They made him look both fierce and harmless, a lion in a cage. (*T* 325)

As well as presenting Edward as a mixture of the brutal and the comedic – both lion and penguin – Farrell also places emphasis on him as a trapped figure, caught here in the 'severe grip' of his suit and caged like a lion. Throughout *Troubles* there emerges a sense of Edward (and by implication all the characters, regardless of their religion, nationality or politics) caged within a historical moment which he strives unsuccessfully to understand, and to which he struggles to respond imaginatively. Edward's increasing eccentricity is a measure of his advancing redundancy, and in it we might read his attempt to cling to a set of values and attitudes which are being overwhelmed by historical events. In the latter stages of the novel he takes to conducting a series of bizarre scientific experiments in his study, one of which involves him firing a shotgun at Murphy, the Irish servant, in order to measure the reduction of saliva in the human mouth when frightened – an event which distresses Murphy considerably. When pressed by the Major as to the purpose, Edward replies distractedly that 'I always wanted to make a contribution, however small' (*T* 310).

Edward is dimly aware that his days at the Majestic are numbered and that the Empire he supports is doomed in Ireland. Yet he clings with increasing absurdity to the values of the world which are slipping away, determined to make his contribution to the 'civilizing', scientific mission of Empire. In representing him as a pathetic figure in both senses of the word – contemptuous but piteous – Farrell suggests that Edward is, like everyone else, 'undergoing history'. He too is caught in the grip of events over which he can exercise little control. Those 'winsomely folded ears' which add a humorous touch of affecting personality to Edward hinder an easy condemnation of him, while underlining how *Troubles* avoids supporting established, separatist ideological positions.

Throughout the Empire Trilogy the British overseas are represented in tones which can be simultaneously harsh and winsome, disapproving and affecting. Some readers have interpreted Farrell's occasionally generous representations of such figures as either nostalgia for a lost Empire or a valorization of discredited colonial attitudes, but closer investigation uncovers a more complex, yet ultimately critical, perspective. Brigid Allen has acknowledged the Empire Trilogy's unquestionable indictment of Imperialism and the wickedness of the British overseas (especially in *The Singapore Grip*). Yet she also makes the important point that 'Jim's light-heartedness saved him from much doctrinaire condemnation; and one feels that he sympathized with the humanity of the British overseas as much as he may have disapproved of them for their transgression'.[8] Throughout the Trilogy, and at the heart of *Troubles*, the depiction of the colonial characters occurs between these conflicting attitudes. Farrell's political reading of Empire contributes to an unsympathetic rendering of the British overseas which highlights their absurdities, destructiveness and iniquity. Yet there is also a degree of identification with them as figures besieged by historical events over which they have no overall control, forced to witness the world, as they have known it, dissolve before their eyes.

Although Farrell might find it difficult to condemn completely the British overseas in his novels, he is much less equivocal about the ideological projects they supported, especially the project of Empire. This is clearly seen in his representation of Irish anti-colonial resistance. Early in the novel, Edward attempts to explain to the Major that the Irish uprising is the work of a small lawless element: 'It was only criminals, fanatics, and certain people with a grudge who were interested in starting trouble. [...] The "decent" Irish (they were ninety-nine per cent according to Edward) were still friendly to the British and as appalled as anyone by the outrages that occurred every now and then' (*T* 73).

Troubles takes several measures to question the validity of Edward's statement. The presence of newspaper extracts plays an important role in challenging the authority of Edward's views, as they construct the historical latticework within which the events in Ireland are contextualised (the Major, significantly, is often glimpsed reading the newspaper). There are three important and overlapping contexts: the British Empire, Bolshevism in Russia, and the First World War. Of the thirty extracts included in the novel, thirteen refer us to troubling events occurring outside Ireland, in such places as Italy, India, Mesopotamia, Russia and South Africa, while others make connections between events in Ireland and the First World War.

Although traumatized by his wartime experiences, the Major believes the war to have been 'a just one [...] throughout the world the great civilising power of the British Empire had been at stake' (*T* 51). As in the confrontation between Edward and the Oxford undergraduates, *Troubles* shows how Irish independence was represented by its opponents as a betrayal of the wartime sacrifices of the troops in the trenches, deemed fighting for the very 'civilised' values under threat in Ireland – an act of 'treachery' epitomized by the Easter Rising in Dublin of 1916. One extract quotes Sir Edward Carson (leader of the protestant Ulster Unionist Council opposed to an Irish Free State) deriding the possibility of an Irish Republic with recourse to an emotive reference to the war: 'I talk of the men sleeping their last sleep on the plains of Flanders and France, in Mesopotamia and Palestine, in the Balkans and elsewhere – the men who have done their share, not for the Irish Republic, but for the great

British Empire' (*T* 91). The overlapping connections between the war, Empire and Irish insurgency are emphasized in a later extract which quotes from Carson's speech in the House of Commons: 'what was going on in Ireland was connected with what was going on in Egypt and India. It was all part of a scheme, openly stated, to reduce Great Britain to the single territory she occupied here, and take from her all the keys of a great Empire' (*T* 175). Although Farrell does not share the tenor of Carson's distress, his novel emphasizes precisely these connections as routes of revolutionary influence.

Other extracts concern eyewitness accounts of 'Bolshevist outrage' and the 'terrorism of the Reds' (*T* 128, 129) as well as Lenin's declaration of war against Poland on behalf of 'the Polish Workers' and Peasants' Republic' (*T* 159). They invite us to think about the indebtedness of Irish resistance to Communist revolution. One rumour which circulates at the Majestic concerns the butler, Murphy, who is reported to have been speaking seditiously at public houses and is 'full of whiskey and Bolshevism' (*T* 187). These extracts suggest that the struggle for Irish independence was, in various ways, indebted to the revolutionary atmosphere of the time, created as a consequence of the Russian revolution and the rise of anti-colonial nationalist groups in other colonized countries. By counterpointing the newspaper extracts with Edward's self-righteous attitudes, Farrell suggests that Edward's view of Irish resistance as the work of a minority of criminals is unsustainable. In addition, Farrell highlights the anti-colonial endeavours of the Irish as part of a much wider political and moral objection to imperious forms of government. In *Troubles*, then, Irish insurgency is represented as an important part of a wider transnational set of resistances to Empire.

On this point, Farrell was arguably well ahead of his time. Only comparatively recently have scholars of colonial and postcolonial culture admitted Ireland into their horizon of study. Postcolonial theory is only just beginning to address the fact that, in Robert Young's words, anti-colonial nationalism was 'constructed and facilitated through international networks of party cells and organizations, and widespread political contacts between different revolutionary organizations that generated common practical information and material support as well as spreading radical political and intellectual ideas'.[9] *Troubles* certainly intimates the existence and importance of these networks. In a recent and excellent essay on *Troubles*, Glenn Hooper has explored at length the transnational elements of the novel, arguing that 'Ireland's role in the general decline of empire is markedly shown, something to which Farrell was acutely sensitive'.[10]

Another reason for *Troubles*'s attention to the First World War concerns its more general interest in the process of writing history. Edward, the Major, Sir Edward Carson and the Oxford undergraduates each make the war meaningful in conflicting and self-interested ways, suggesting that history is as malleable and illusory as the stories we can make about it. On his first morning at the Majestic the Major listens to Edward discoursing at breakfast on those killed in the war. His eye is drawn to a wooden memorial for the fallen who, in Edward's words, 'gave their lives for their King, their country and for us' (*T* 47). The memorial significantly resembles the pages of a book and contains photographs of the dead. The Major gloomily reflects that 'There were so many ways in which the vast army of the dead could be drilled, classified, inspected, and made to present their ghostly arms' (*T* 46). Although barely over, the lost lives of this 'vast army' are becoming little more than emotive evidence for the propriety and legitimacy of Empire and 'civilisation'. The photographs are less meaningful than a book in which they appear, which locates the soldiers' lost lives within an imperious narrative of 'our glorious dead'. As a veteran of the war, the Major can see through such documents of civilization to the troubling barbarity and wreckage which they conceal. Edward's history book does not record the experience of trenches which has left the Major shell-shocked and many of his friends slain; only the 'magnificent sacrifice' of their slaughter. The Major, like the novel, sees such haughty convictions as merely rhetoric.

As a writer concerned with the realm of experience that the conventional historian leaves out, Farrell makes the questioning of the narration of history – its inclusions and exclusions, its stories and silences – an important theme of the novel. This is precisely because the justification of Empire depends upon the manufacture of sanitized versions of the past which leave out the pain and violence suffered by those undergoing history (on all sides, of course). On several similar occasions the novel highlights the existence of a troubled relationship between writing and experience, often with particular reference to the Major. Before travelling to the Majestic for the first time, the Major is confident that he knows the place very well through Angela's many letters with which he 'embroidered for himself a colourful tapestry of Angela's life at the Majestic' (*T* 13). But on arrival in Ireland he is disconcerted to be met at Kilnalough station by Angela's brother Ripon – whom Angela never mentioned before – and soon realizes that there is a considerable difference between his fiancée and the woman he had come to imagine through her letters: 'he only half remembered her; she was half herself and half some stranger, but neither half belonged to the image he had had of her while reading her weekly letter (*T* 21–22). Representation and reality seem disjunctive here, with writing deemed increasingly unreliable and remote from the things it is meant to represent faithfully.

A similar point is forcibly made later in the novel when the Major attends the Peace Day parade in Dublin and witnesses an assassination of an old man. He reads about it in the newspaper the following day and pauses for reflection:

> It was as if these newspaper articles were poultices placed on sudden inflammations of violence. In a day or two all the poison had been drawn out of them. They became random events of the year 1919, inevitable, without malice, part of history. The old man lying on the bridge with his watch in his hand was a part of history. [...] A raid on a barracks, the murder of a policeman on a lonely country road, an airship crossing the Atlantic, a speech by a man on a platform, or any of the other random acts, mostly violent, that one reads about every day: this was the history of the time. The rest was merely the 'being alive' that every age has to do. (*T* 102)

This famous passage certainly relates to Farrell's concerns with the inadequacy of conventional history and his desire to represent people 'undergoing history', all the minutiae of 'being alive' which is not normally recorded. It also beckons an important historiographical self-consciousness into the text. Like all histories, *Troubles* can only be a partial, selective, limited representation of a period which it can never adequately portray. The 'being alive' of every age ultimately remains beyond its horizon of possibility, just as the poisonous violence of conflict can never be adequately conveyed in language (such as Edward's wooden war memorial). In calling attention to the act of writing history, and delineating the disjunction between writing and 'being alive', *Troubles* is at such moments distinctly postmodernist in its attitudes, troubled about the creative processes in which it is involved. The 'history of the time' recorded in newspapers and other such documents can only ever be a selective and inadequate version of events which cannot fully convey the 'senseless act' (*T* 102) witnessed by the Major. Farrell's version, written in the late 1960s, is at a further remove from the 'being alive' of the age, and the novel is at pains to point out the inadequacy and unreliability of its own vista.

The Major's dissatisfaction with newspaper reports is also an index of the declining fortunes of the British in Ireland. Although the Major is not of the Anglo-Irish Ascendancy and does not seem so violently opposed to the Irish, as a former officer in the British Army he is certainly complicit with the British presence in Ireland and his attitudes to the Irish are by no means progressive. His increasing inability to comprehend what is going on around him portrays a failure of imagination on the part of the British in Ireland. We have seen how the newspaper reports clearly link Irish insurgency with other important contexts, but the Major cannot make these connections. Instead he declares himself defeated by a seemingly nonsensical situation. For the Major, whose experience of war in the trenches has given him a certain sense of how battles should be fought, the tactics of the IRA leave him bemused:

> The news from Ireland was dull and dispiriting: an occasional attack on a lonely policeman or a raid for arms on some half-baked barracks. If one was not actually living in Ireland (as the lucky Major no longer was) how could one possibily take an interest when, for instance, at the same time Negroes and white men were fighting it out in the streets of Chicago? Now *that* gripped the Major's imagination more forcibly. Unlike the Irish troubles one knew instantly which side everyone was on. In the Chicago race-riots people were using their skins like uniforms. (*T* 113).

There are several such moments in *Troubles* when the Major gives up trying to comprehend events: 'in Ireland, the troubles ebbed and flowed, now better, now worse. He could make no sense of it' (*T* 138); 'The Major only glanced at the newspaper these days, tired of trying to comprehend a situation which defied comprehension, a war without battles or trenches' (*T* 169). These moments suggest something of the novelty of the IRA's guerrilla tactics under the leadership of Michael Collins, favouring ambushes and assassinations as part of a murderous and highly effective campaign of terror against the British and 'disloyal' Irishmen.[11] They also suggest that one part of the demise of British authority in Ireland was the gradual loss of the ability to understand history. As the British lose their political control in Ireland, they suffer the loss of their power as historians to select, narrate and give meaning to events. The Major's difficulties in understanding history are of the same nature as Edward's increasing sense of redundancy which we considered earlier, and he too struggles to respond to the changing situation around him. Furthermore, if the power to narrate history is seen as an index of political authority, then it is perhaps no surprise that *Troubles* occasionally approaches a postmodernist self-consciousness of its own limits as a historical representation: to presume to depict a confident, omnipotent and reliable version of events in Ireland would risk complicity with the imperious certainties of the British overseas which the novel is at pains to undercut.

If Farrell clearly wishes to travesty the ideological attitudes of the British overseas – however sympathetic he is to their predicament 'undergoing history' – he is perhaps problematically equivocal when it comes to the representation of the Irish. Farrell's Irish characters tend a little towards cliché and stereotype; indeed, the representation of colonised peoples throughout the Empire Trilogy remains a vexed issue. The representation of the Protestant Irish is certainly unflattering. At the Majestic the Major encounters Edward's solicitor, Mr O'Neill, an Ulsterman who does little else but spout objectionable rhetoric about the Catholic Irish and whose yellowish face suggests he has cancer. At Edward's ball, the narrator remarks upon the assembled 'quality' in the following terms:

> This was the face of Anglo-Ireland, the inbred Protestant aristocracy, the face, progressively refining itself into a separate, luxurious species, which had ruled Ireland for almost five hundred years: the wispy fair hair, the eyes too close together, the long nose and protruding teeth. 'Ripon was right [reflected the Major], in a biological sense as well as several others, to marry Máire Noonan.' (*T* 336)

Although Farrell's opposition to the Anglo-Irish Ascendancy's authority might be justifiable in political terms, it is a little disingenuous to translate such objections into a prejudiced and derogatory statement about a separate 'species' with 'peculiar' features. The Catholic Irish fare little better. The Majestic features two important servants: the cook and the butler, Murphy. The unnamed cook suffers a highly unflattering depiction in *Troubles*, as at the moment when the Major asks her about Angela's failure to appear at dinner: 'Her face was working with emotion; between volleys of words there were shuddering intakes of breath; her shoulders shook, causing the gelatinous layers of flesh on her arms to shiver. '"Good heavens!" thought the Major with concern. "What can it all be about?"' (*T* 53). Fat and incomprehensible, the cook is little else but a buffoon. Monstrous in size and similarly incomprehensible to the Major, Murphy is a sinister figure more familiar to the pages of gothic literature. It is he who razes the Majestic to the ground and appears at the end of the novel among the flames, 'a hideous, cadaverous figure [. . .] his clothes a cloak of fire, his hair ablaze: Satan himself' (*T* 443). Although there may be a degree of irony in this description, like the cook Murphy is always an incomprehensible, inscrutable and unsettling presence for those at the Majestic. We are not taken inside these characters' worlds. According to Margaret Scanlan, 'a restricted narrative view shuts out the Catholic Irish and, thereby, becomes complicit in their dehumanisation by the British'.[12] Although it is implied that we are seeing such figures through the limited eyes of the Major, the novel's narrator struggles to challenge or undercut such problematic visions.

Sarah Devlin is a particularly troubling figure. At one level she is clearly connected to Irish republican politics, pointedly reminding those at the Majestic of the divisions between Catholics and Protestants as well as highlighting the bigotry of the Anglo-Irish, happy to denigrate Catholics as '"fish-eaters" and "Holy Romans" and so on' (*T* 34). She has a directness and cheerfully disruptive manner which combats the anti-Irish attitudes of Edward, Mr O'Neill and others. We first see her sitting in a wheelchair trying to pick an apple with a pair of walking-sticks, suggesting perhaps Ireland's incapacitated condition under British rule. While languishing in London the

Major receives a letter from Sarah in which she tells him about being courted by a 'rural swain' (*T* 118). Although uninterested in his advances, Sarah is impressed by a gold ring he wears in his lapel as a member of An Fáinne: 'a circle for Irish-speaking people' who no longer wish to communicate in the language 'of the foreigner' (*T* 118). Sarah regards this as 'a wonderful idea' (*T* 118). Yet Farrell does not really develop Sarah as a symbol of Ireland, and she soon becomes as inscrutable and baffling to the Major as Murphy and the cook.

The Major's amorous pursuit of Sarah is thwarted by her capricious, secretive and unpredictable nature. Her affair with Edward severely questions the integrity and depth of her political beliefs, while her elopement with Captain Bolton, one of the unsavoury British soldiers staying at the Majestic, is perhaps the biggest surprise of all. The Major learns that 'if she so much as looks at another man [Bolton] knocks her cold on the spot' (*T* 388). It is difficult to know how best to read this detail. On the one hand Farrell may be making a comment about Britain's sadistic investment in Ireland, both possessive and violent. On the other hand, he might be looking ahead to the continuing violent relations between Britain and Ireland, especially in the six counties of Northern Ireland, at the time the novel was written. Although this reading only works if we accept Sarah as allegorical of the nation (itself a questionable manoeuvre). Yet neither reading is especially convincing, and one wonders whether this detail risks a little misogyny. Is her affair with Bolton the ultimate evidence of Sarah's own inconstant attractions to the cruelty of the class she seems to despise?

When we recall that the only survivor of the Majestic's razing is the statue of Venus, an abstracted image of love which recalls the vision of Inez as Botticelli's Venus in *A Girl in the Head*, one wonders whether in *Troubles* Sarah is the 'fallen' half of the angel–whore opposition which appears in the previous novel in the contrast between Inez and Lady Jane. The Major's fiancée, Angela, recalls the figure of the angel in her name, while the Major stupidly accuses Sarah of being 'a dirty whore' (*T* 374) when he discovers her affair with Edward at the ball. It is discouraging to discover that some of the problems which marred *A Girl in the Head* are still present in its illustrious and far superior successor.

In writing *Troubles*, Farrell made some vital steps forward. In choosing public events as the subject of the novel he displaced some of the gloomy, despairing and melancholic moods which overshadowed his early life and novels, allowing the tremulous laughter of his best early work to develop in complex, important ways. His parodic approach to literary genre gave him important formal structures within which he could work playfully and with increasing confidence, while his attention to the theme of the decline and fall of colonialism gave both rhythm and shape to his fiction. In the next two novels Farrell would write in the light of the example of *Troubles*. In each the method is surer, the design more established. Yet *Troubles* perhaps remains the most hypnotic and powerful of the Trilogy not least because it is, for Farrell, his novel of discovery: of a literary style, of a critical attitude to Empire, and of a pointed laughter, the vitality of which increasingly comes to characterize his vision.

4

India, 1857 & 1871

On the day following the publication of *The Siege of Krishnapur* in August 1973, an interview between J. G. Farrell and his friend Malcolm Dean appeared in the *Guardian* newspaper under the title 'An Insight Job'. Farrell explained that in his new book he had attempted 'to write a novel of ideas which could be read at the same time simply as an adventure story'.[1] His choice of setting – India in 1857, the year of the 'Indian Mutiny'[2] – afforded him a propitious opportunity to dovetail each fictional concern. In Farrell's view nineteenth-century British India 'was a society with rules and an idealism of its own'.[3] *The Siege of Krishnapur* attempts to engage comically and critically with the ideas, and idealism, of the time, especially the colonial self-confidence in Western civilization, faith, scientific advancement and, of course, Empire. In addition, there existed a popular tradition of British writing about adventures in India by such figures as Rudyard Kipling and John Masters, and specifically about the Mutiny, upon which Farrell could draw in a way similar to his appropriation of the Big House novel in *Troubles*.

The Siege of Krishnapur ironically resurrects the voice and concerns of nineteenth-century English fiction in its depiction of the Mutiny. As Peter Morey explains, the novel 'attempts not only cultural retrieval by using the popular nineteenth-century genre of imperial adventure fiction, but also its subversion through a technique of ironic distancing, pastiche and the mock-heroic'.[4] It is also an exercise in fictional rule-breaking, challenging the conventional ways in which colonial India has been narrated. Farrell's approach is deliberately comic, and the comic vision he creates of the British in India is central to the novel's critical purposes. But as we shall see, at times the novel risks complicity with the very colonialist representations Farrell wishes to ironize and challenge. In *The Siege of Krishnapur* the 'novel of ideas' occasionally sits uneasily alongside the 'adventure story' it makes of the events of 1857.

The Indian Mutiny concerned the uprising of the 'native' troops, or 'sepoys', of the Bengal Army. The sepoys were subject to the authority of often discriminatory British commanding officers who cared little for their religions and cultures. A growing sense of grievance came to a head in 1857 when rumours began to spread that the new consignments of Enfield rifles issued to the sepoys required a different kind of cartridge that was heavily greased with tallow. When loading the rifle, the end of the cartridge needed to be bitten off in order for the powder it contained to ignite when the rifle was fired. As tallow often contained beef or pig fat, the prospect of biting the cartridge was, to the Indian troops, abhorrent, as Christopher Hibbert explains: 'if [the cartridge] contained beef fat it would be degrading to Hindus and if it contained pig fat it would be offensive to Mohammedans [Muslims]'.[5] In May, a troop of Indians in Meerut refused to use the new cartridges, and eighty-five were imprisoned as punishment. Soon after, the Indians in Meerut revolted, burning homes and killing Europeans. Similar violence quickly spread to Delhi, Dinapore, Gwalior, Muttra, Cawnpore and Lucknow.

If the Mutiny was bloody and violent, so too was the punishment meted out by the British. Sepoys captured or found guilty of mutiny were hanged, sometimes in pigskin hoods if Muslims, or blown from the cannons. In September British forces recaptured Delhi, and the remaining mutineers were defeated by Spring 1858. The Mutiny was widely reported in the British press which often exaggerated the violence of the sepoys and portrayed Indians as bloodthirsty barbarians. To much of Victorian society in Britain, events in India seemed inconceivable. As Denis Judd explains, 'The Indian Mutiny was consequently interpreted as an unwarranted and destructive rejection of British reforming benevolence, and an assault on the very notion of progress'.[6] Both the activities and the *idea* of Empire seemed under attack, as Farrell's critical fictionalization of the conflict also makes clear.

The Siege of Krishapur is based quite closely upon the siege of Lucknow. Indian regiments stationed at Lucknow mutinied on

May 30, forcing Europeans to retreat into the Residency where they remained besieged under terrible conditions until relief began to arrive on September 25, although Lucknow was not recaptured until March 1858. Farrell stayed in Lucknow in February 1971 as part of a three-month research trip to India. His novel concerns the fortunes of a variety of expatriate colonials living in or near the British Residency at the fictional setting of Krishnapur. Mr Hopkins, known as the Collector, functions as the administrative head of the Krishnapur cantonment. An enthusiast of the 1851 Great Exhibition in London, he is in one regard representative of the self-confidence and conviction of the 'civilising mission' of nineteenth-century British colonialism and, to an extent, plays a similar role to that of Edward Spencer in *Troubles*. Yet the Collector is ultimately a more sympathetic and complex figure who tries to reflect critically upon the problems of colonialism – there is more than a touch of the Major about him too. At the beginning of the novel the Collector appears simultaneously as a foreboding and slightly comical figure via a typically Farrellian simile: he dresses fastidiously with unusually high collars and carefully trims his side-whiskers 'which nevertheless sprouted out stiffly like the ruff of a cat' (*SK* 11).

Other significant figures of authority include the Magistrate, an enthusiastic advocate of phrenology, and the Padre. Two families are also important: the Dunstables and the Fleurys. Dr Dunstable is Krishnapur's civil surgeon and one of two British doctors stationed in Krishnapur (the other is Dr McNab, the regimental surgeon). His son, Harry, is an ensign in an Indian infantry regiment stationed close by at Captainganj, while his daughter, Louise, is considered in society to be a particularly beautiful and eligible young woman. Recently arrived in India are George Fleury (known by his surname throughout the novel) and his sister Miriam, whose father holds the eminent position of Director in the prestigious East India Company. The Fleurys are in India for a particular reason: George has been commissioned by the Company to write a short volume on the 'advances that civilisation had made in India under the Company rule' (*SK* 22), but the real reason behind their visit is to divert the spirits of Miriam, who has been recently widowed. Louise attracts the attentions of Fleury during a party in

Calcutta where she and Harry are spending the 'cold season'. Once the characters relocate in Krishnapur in April 1857, she finds herself the object of his amorous pursuits.

At the beginning of the novel the Collector is filled with foreboding on finding four chapatis which mysteriously appear in a despatch box on his desk. At first his sense of impending doom is an object of scorn, but he is soon vindicated as the Indian sepoys begin to revolt throughout the region. Soon the British find themselves besieged inside the cantonment and under serious attack. Further characters are introduced. One figure is Lucy Hughes: a disgraced, 'fallen' British woman whom Harry and Fleury are delighted to rescue from the town and whose presence does much to disconcert several of the 'respectable' ladies in the cantonment. Two other important characters are the local Maharajah and his son, Hari, who has been educated by English tutors and is fascinated with Western science and invention, especially photography. As the siege worsens, the Collector imprisons the Maharajah and Hari in an attempt to deter Indian attacks, much to Hari's consternation. The bulk of the novel features the endeavours of the British to defend the cantonment from attack, a process which is vividly rendered in a series of bizarre scenes. Slowly they find themselves stripped of the possessions which they highly prize. The luxurious material trappings of the Residency – 'Sofas and tables, beds, chests, dressers and hatstands' (*SK* 244) – are appropriated to shore up the ramparts which protect the cantonment and are used as ammunition for the cannons as supplies run low. On one occasion a cannon loaded with the marble fragments of statues, cutlery, lightning conductors and other bric-à-brac is fired at the sepoys, with devastating consequences; on another, a statue of Shakespeare's head proves its 'ballistic advantages' (*SK* 304) as ammunition. Food supplies run low and rationing is introduced, so that presently the British come to resemble 'tattered skeletons' (*SK* 252).

More importantly perhaps, several characters also find themselves stripped of the certainties, values and ideals to which they have been ardently committed. Whereas most of the characters ultimately survive the 'adventure' of being besieged (relief arrives eventually in October), some of their ideas do not. In later life, back in Britain, the Collector withdraws from society and spends much of his time brooding in the poor areas of London and reading newspapers. At the end of the novel he encounters Fleury (who has since married Louise and started a family) and tells him that 'Culture is a sham, [...] a cosmetic painted on life by rich people to conceal its ugliness' (*SK* 313). Fleury remains to be convinced and is still happy to espouse nineteenth-century ideals of progress and the quest for 'higher life' (*SK* 313). Yet the Collector has the last word: 'he had come to believe that a people, a nation, does not create itself according to its own best ideas, but is shaped by other forces, of which it has little knowledge' (*SK* 313).

In a similar fashion to *Troubles*, *The Siege of Krishnapur* attends to the experiences of the overseas British 'undergoing history', trying to cope with an historical situation which directly challenges the values which underwrite and motivate their lives. The besieged Residency echoes the crumbling Majestic hotel, while the slow disintegration of the cantonment and increasingly desperate conditions suffered by the British repeat the atmosphere of decline and fall. At the beginning of the novel the Residency stands as the concrete manifestation of all that is deemed superior and noble in European civilization, not least because of the possessions it houses. The splendid library, the paintings and furniture, the electro-magnetic statuettes of 'Dr Johnson, of Molière, Keats, Voltaire and, of course, Shakespeare' (*SK* 16) are all evidence to the Collector of the 'superior morality' (*SK* 80) of Western progress. But by the end the Collector notes that the Greek pillars of the banqueting hall, pocked and shattered by shot, are not marble as he has assumed: 'He lingered for a moment sneering at the guilty red core that was revealed beneath the stucco of lime and sand. He hated pretence' (*SK* 302). This moment of revelation stands as a useful image of the novel's intention to disclose nineteenth-century ideas about Western modernity and civilization as a façade which obscures the bloody brutality of colonialism.

As is the case throughout the Empire Trilogy, Farrell places the textuality of history at its heart. *The Siege of Krishapur* is full of references to textual production – documents, photographs, literary works, chronicles – and a number of its characters are budding writers. In the opening chapter we witness a meeting of the Krishnapur Poetry Society in which Miss Carpenter reads her poetic celebration of the Great Exhibition of 1851; Fleury is also an aspiring poet as well as involved in writing his book for the Company; Dr McNab keeps a journal of his medical efforts as the siege worsens. The novel also features an 'Afterword' in which Farrell declares that much of his fiction relies upon 'the mass of diaries, letters and memoirs written by eyewitnesses, in some cases with the words of the witness only slightly modified; certain of my characters also had their beginnings in this material' (SK 314). His admitted appropriation of these texts maintains the important self-consciousness concerning history's provisionality and subjectivity first mooted in *Troubles*. It is worth noting that the production of knowledge about Britain and India at the time is one of the novel's important themes from the very beginning. Farrell is fascinated by the *language* of Empire, the ways in which the British represented their colonial achievements to themselves. At the heart of the Residency is the 'vernacular record room' which houses a wealth of documentation concerning the British administration of Krishnapur:

> Its walls were lined from floor to ceiling with tier over tier of stone shelves; to protect the records from white ants they were tied up in bundles of cotton cloth brilliantly dyed in different colours for ease of reference ... and these bright colours gave the shelves the gay appearance of flowerbeds. This cloth protection, however, was not always effective and sometimes when he opened a bundle the Magistrate would find himself looking, not at the document he required, but at a little heap of powdery earth. And then he would give a shout of bitter laughter which echoed across the compound and had more than once caused the Collector to raise his eyebrows. [...] In India all official proceedings, even the most trivial, were conducted in writing, and so the rapidity with which the piles of paper grew was alarming and ludicrous. (SK 100 101)

The 'piles of paper' which accumulate in the vernacular record are part of the different accounts – literary as well as documentary – that will become the period's historical documents. Their disintegration into 'powdery earth' anticipates the ways in which *The Siege of Krishnapur* attempts to fragment the values embedded in the record of the Mutiny in particular and British colonialism in general. It also acknowledges the incomplete and unreliable character of all historical archives. There is the suggestion in the papers' demise that British 'civilisation' cannot be successfully transplanted to or imposed upon India. The 'bitter laugh' of the Magistrate is, perhaps, recognition of the precariousness of British authority, and also suggests the ultimate goal of the novel as a whole: the creation of a bitter laughter which rewrites the 'sanity' of nineteenth-century colonialism in India as ludicrousness. The novel's self-consciousness about the volatility of the historical archive reminds us that *The Siege of Krishnapur* is a late-twentieth-century critical anatomization of the Mutiny and, first and foremost, a strategic *re-writing* of history.

Like the fake marble columns in the Residency, Farrell exposes the self-confident language of Empire as an illusion which attempts to conceal a 'guilty red core' of brutality and bloodshed. The image of the heroic male who secures his masculine identity and earns rich rewards by fighting for Queen and Empire is consistently unmasked in several of the novel's more sober moments. One powerful example concerns an incident in the Residency's makeshift hospital. The description of the Collector's tour of the injured and wounded is punctuated by an anonymous English soldier's ballad which he is singing to maintain his spirits:

> I'm ax'd for a song and 'mong soldiers 'tis plain,
> I'd best sing a battle, a siege or campaign.
> Of victories to choose from we Britons have store,
> And need but to go back to eigh*teen* fifty-four. (*SK* 163)

The reference is to the Crimean War of 1854, and the soldier's song celebrates the valour and 'fair play' of the 'brave boys' (*SK* 167) who fought so gloriously in defence of Queen and Empire. But the song sounds to the Collector both monotonous and 'desperate' (*SK* 167). When set in the context of the hospital, with its 'stench of putrefaction and chloroform' (*SK* 161) and full of those dreadfully wounded in the outbreak of hostilities, the soldier's song seems to be remote from the realities of battle. Certainly those British soldiers in the hospital who have just escaped the Mutiny at Captainganj 'did not seem to be thinking of it as an adventure. [...] Each of them simply had two or three terrible scenes printed on his mind: an Englishwoman trying to say something to him with her throat cut, or a comrade spinning down into a whirlpool of hacking sepoys, something of that sort'

(*SK* 94–95). In Farrell's hands, the Mutiny affords the opportunity to question rather than confirm heroic representations of British colonialism. It is with bitter irony that the General who leads the liberation of Krishnapur at the novel's conclusion recognizes the profoundly un-heroic appearance of the siege's survivors, as well as the necessity to maintain the heroic fiction of the British in India:

> Even when allowances where made, the 'heroes of Krishnapur', as [the General] did not doubt they would soon be called, were a pretty rum lot. And he would have to pose for hours, holding a sword and perched on a trestle or wooden horse while some artist-wallah depicted 'The Relief of Krishnapur'! He must remember to insist on being foregrounded, however; then it would not be so bad. With luck this wretched selection of 'heroes' would be given the soft pedal ... an indistinct crowd of corpses and a few grateful faces, cannons and prancing horses would be best. (*SK* 310–311)

The novel's final depiction of the besieged Residency is refracted through the General's imagination, which calls attention to the production of images of valour in representations of the Mutiny. The 'rum lot' who have 'undergone' history and survived the siege riddled with disease and emaciated by hunger, as well as those who did not, will become only part of the background as their presence contradicts the image of British valour epitomized by the posing General. It is the heroic image of the Mutiny which both celebrates and falsifies British endeavour that *The Siege of Krishnapur* wishes to unsettle. As Jenny Sharpe has argued, 'our perception of 1857 has been coloured by the years of myth-making that have gone into the popularised revolt'.[7] Farrell endeavours to reveal the hypocrisy of such myth-making that lays claim to historical 'authenticity' by prising apart the heroic language of Empire's 'adventures' from the bloody realities it masks.

This is a solemn task perhaps, yet Farrell's preferred fictional method, as ever, is frequently comic. As Ralph Crane and Jennifer Livett suggest, '*The Siege of Krishnapur* transforms the adventure story into a richly, darkly, ironic account of the British Raj in the mid-Victorian period'.[8] In particular, Farrell drew upon the late-nineteenth-century popular genre of 'Mutiny' novels which eulogized the British defeat of the sepoys.

Remarkably similar in structure, such texts depicted a young, adventurous male hero who, against all the odds, assists in quelling the Mutiny and ultimately wins the hand of a beloved. As S. D. Singh explains, the twinned plots of adventure and romance are two of the genre's most characteristic features:

> The fictionalisation of history demands a romantic situation to go alongside the historical situation of the mutiny [...]. The two parallel plots of action are resolved by the hero, who, in most of the cases, gets a V.C., as well as a wife, if not also an estate and a title to lord it over at home in England.[9]

The Siege of Krishnapur ironically uses the conventions of the 'Mutiny novel' for the purposes of comic critique, as can be seen in the characterization and fortunes of George Fleury. In contrast to the valiant heroes of the 'Mutiny novel', Fleury is a bookish, sensitive and impractical figure who seems rather out of place in India among the conventionally gallant males who crave adventure rather than poetry and music. He 'generally liked sad things, such as autumn, death, ruins and unhappy love affairs' (*SK* 26) and paid 'little heed to physical and sporting matters' (*SK* 36), much to the distress of his father. His naivety is both comical and alarming, and he seems ill-prepared for the realities of the Indian landscape. On arriving at the bazaar in Krishnapur, Fleury is amazed at the crowds he witnesses: 'Where could they all possibly live? An incongruous picture came into Fleury's mind of a hundred and fifty people squatting of [sic] the floor of his aunt's drawing-room in Torquay' (*SK* 43)

Farrell creates much of the novel's comedy through Fleury's habitually inappropriate conduct throughout the novel. He regards an early sepoy attack as an opportunity to write 'an epic poem' (*SK* 138), while he responds to the death of Mary Porter from sunstroke by 'composing a poem in which her little ghost came tripping along the ramparts sniffing flowers, unperturbed by the flying cannon balls (it was not a very good poem) (*SK* 220). In battle he is – at least to begin with – similarly ineffective. During one incident when Harry and Fleury are manning one of the cantonment's cannons and are about to be over-run by a sepoy assault, Fleury is caught daydreaming:

> 'Fleury, for God's sake!' shouted Harry, who knew how desperate the situation was. Fleury did not know; he was in a daze from the

noise and smoke which had tears streaming down his face, and the haze of dust which hung everywhere, very fine, lending the scene a 'historical' quality because everything appeared faintly blurred, as in a Crimean daguerrotype. Fleury found himself appending captions to himself for the *Illustrated London News*. 'This was the Banqueting Hall Redoubt in the Battle of Krishnapur. On the left, Mr Fleury, the poet, who conducted himself so gallantly throughout; on the right, Lieutenant Dunstable, who commanded the Battery, and a faithful native, Ram.' (*SK* 139)

In his quest to act out his fantasy of the poet-hero, Fleury is an often ineffectual presence who needs to be rescued from disaster (often by Harry) on more than one occasion.

However, Farrell's ironical engagement with the romantic and heroic conventions of the 'Mutiny' adventure story only goes so far. To be sure, Fleury is often an absurd figure whose prowess in battle leaves much to be desired, but he is not a total failure in conflict. In one incident, he rides into battle sporting an invention he has termed the 'Fleury Cavalry Eradicator' which 'resembled a giant pitchfork with prongs roughly at a distance of a man's outstretched arms; it also had a wide tail, like that of a magnified bishop's crozier which, reversed, could be used for dragging people off horses' (*SK* 183). Fleury is convinced that his Eradicator will revolutionize cavalry charges by allowing its user to attack two of the enemy simultaneously. The Eradicator satirizes the enthusiasm for new inventions beloved of the Collector, and its comic effect is accentuated by the fact that it makes Fleury's horse appear to possess a pair of 'weird antlers' (*SK* 184).

The Eradicator is a spectacular failure: when deploying it Fleury realizes that he has miscalculated the distance between its prongs and then finds himself unceremoniously whisked out of the saddle to hang 'like a gaffed salmon on [its] end' (*SK* 185). It is one of several such moments in the novel where the prospect of valour becomes an opportunity for bathos and laughter. Yet this particular incident ends with Fleury successfully spiking one of the sepoys' guns, and when Lieutenant Peterson is fatally wounded both Fleury and Harry do not hesitate to come to his aid at considerable risk to their own safety. Although there remains the suggestion that Fleury still attempts to act more like a sentimental poet – he tries to remove Peterson's locket to give to Peterson's wife – at this point he seems much more in keeping with the conventional hero of the 'Mutiny' adventure story. So when the narrator remarks that 'Fleury came very well out of this attack. He and Harry had both behaved with great bravery in full view of everyone' (*SK* 187) the degree of irony intended here is not absolutely clear.

On more than one occasion *The Siege of Krishnapur* seems to switch like this from an ironical to a conventional colonial adventure story. This is, inevitably, a risk created by any parodic strategy, since such narratives have to install the very conventions which are to be satirized. Thus, complicity in those conventions is an inevitable consequence of building critique. Yet the level of complicity occasionally appears high, so that at times *The Siege of Krishnapur* indulges, rather than undermines, a heroic representation of the Mutiny. In particular, the character of Harry is frequently presented as a resourceful and quick-witted individual whose valour saves the day on more than one occasion. This compromises the extent to which *The Siege of Krishnapur* can be considered an anti-colonial, or even post-colonial, novel. In one incident near the end of the novel Fleury becomes involved in hand-to-hand combat with a sepoy in the music room. At first the incident is slapstick and farcical: Fleury's gun refuses to fire and his daggers become caught in his belt. An attempt to swing from a chandelier and kick the sepoy in the face is scuppered when the chandelier refuses to bear his weight. Desperately, Fleury strangles the sepoy with violin strings but this also fails to repel his foe. At the very moment when it seems Fleury is about to be killed, he stumbles upon his gun and fires it again. This time it works:

> Indeed not just one barrel fired, but all fifteen; they were not supposed to, but that was what happened. He found himself confronted now by a midriff and a pair of legs; the wall behind the legs was draped in scarlet. The top half of the sepoy had vanished. So it seemed to Fleury in his excitement, anyway. (*SK* 295).

The last sentence in this quotation attempts to displace the narrator from Fleury's sense of 'excitement' perhaps, yet it seems too little, too late. The 'excitement' created by the incident invites the reader to celebrate Fleury's good fortune and breathe a sigh of relief, and any thoughts for the nameless sepoy conveniently vanish. Like Fleury, the novel at times becomes an over-willing participant of adventure and seems to enjoy the 'excitement' it creates. The laughter created by its comical representation of the Mutiny can occasionally be one of relief rather than criticism.

In its attempted critique of the macho heroism of colonial adventure, *The Siege of Krishnapur* importantly questions the construction of gender roles and the conventions they inscribe. When Lucy Hughes, the 'fallen woman', takes shelter in the Residency as the cantonment burns she precipitates a new crisis:

> In spite of the harrowing circumstances the ladies were still refusing to have anything to do with her ... they had hissed with indignation at the suggestion that she should sleep in the billiard room where ladies of the better class had been installed. But where else could she sleep? The Collector's authority had been invoked in the end and she had duly been established there, but nobody was happy about the arrangement. (*SK* 134)

The 'harrowing circumstances' of the siege expose gendered ideas of social propriety as prejudicial and asinine. Sexist attitudes towards women are seen as part of the folly of the British in India. Fleury believes that 'a woman's special skill is to listen quietly to what a fellow has to say and thereby create the sort of atmosphere in which good conversation can flourish' (*SK* 49). Both Fleury and Harry have an absurdly idealistic notion of women which is exposed in the incident when Lucy is attacked by a cloud of black cockchafers which envelope her body. In a panic she rips off her clothes but this makes little difference: the insects continue to swarm over her. Coming gallantly to the rescue, Fleury and Harry scrape off the insects with the boards torn from a Bible. They are pleased to notice that her body resembles the statues of women they have seen, but soon are made to think twice:

> The only significant difference between Lucy and a statue was that Lucy had pubic hair; this caused them a bit of a surprise at first. It was not something that had ever occurred to [Fleury and Harry] as possible, likely, or even, desirable.
> 'D'you think this is *supposed* to be here?' asked Harry [...].
> 'That's odd,' said Fleury, peering at it with interest; he had never seen anything like it on a statue. 'Better leave it, anyway, for the time being. We can always come back to it later when we've done the rest.' (*SK* 232)

The nineteenth-century construction of the passive, silent, idealized women is vividly contested in the figure of Miriam Dunstable. Like Martin Sands and the Major – and, of course, Farrell – she has been brought face to face with death at a young age (she is widowed) and displays a muted stoicism in the novel. As the siege progresses, Miriam becomes an increasingly important figure, and often acts as an understated yet important critical voice on proceedings. During her nursing of the Collector through a painful illness, he reminds her to think of her reputation lest others form impressions of their relationship. She responds by calling into question the rules and regulations of society in a manner which underlines the design of the novel as a whole: 'After all this, Mr Hopkins, do you think that reputations still matter?' (SK 227). She also becomes disillusioned with the gendering of society and feels trapped by its protocols: 'Miriam was tired of womanhood. She wanted simply to experience life as an anonymous human being of flesh and blood. She was tired of having to adjust to other people's ideas of what a woman should be' (SK 218). Miriam's 'tiredness' acts as a critical lever on the attitudes of many of the cantonment's ladies and the macho gallantry ardently pursued by Fleury and Harry.

Fleury's 'Cavalry Eradicator' is one of a number of remarkable objects referred to in the novel. Several characters regard the material belongings at the Residency as tangible evidence of British advancement and superiority, and their presence often prompts an exploration of the ideas they are made to symbolize. In the Collector's study appear two prized objects: '*The Spirit of Science Conquers Ignorance and Prejudice*, a bas-relief in marble by the window' and a sculpture titled '*Innocence Protected by Fidelity* by Benzoni, representing a scantily clothed young girl, asleep with a garland of flowers in her lap; beside her a dog had its paw on the neck of a gagging snake which had been about to bite her' (SK 87). Each object is made to cast an ironic shadow in the novel. The first epitomizes the faith in science and technology as promising advancement and enlightenment. Yet the novel shows that such initiatives instead serve the ignorance and prejudice of the British in India who regard their possessions as evidence of advancement and superiority. This point is forcefully underlined during the siege when, due to the ammunition shortage, *The Spirit of Science* is shot from a cannon and shatters a sepoy's spine. Benzoni's sculpture anticipates the forthcoming siege, as well as portraying the defence of 'innocence' in conventionally gendered terms. Throughout the novel material objects fulfil a dual purpose. To adapt Walter Benjamin's famous phrase: if the Residency, the cantonment buildings and the possessions begin the novel as monuments of civilization, they eventually come to signify the barbarity of the British in India – ignorant and contemptuous of Indian life, and arrogantly self-confident. The colonial settlers' cultural, intellectual and technological 'treasures' are exposed as being at the service of an often brutal and violent regime.

The Collector's title refers to his fascination with artistic and scientific objects, and he enthusiastically attended the Great Exhibition at London's Crystal Palace in 1851. He has brought to India 'examples of European art and science in the belief that he was doing as once the Romans had done in Britain' which makes the Residency 'full of statues, paintings and machines' (*SK* 34). The Collector is a firm believer in progress and regards material innovation as the means by which humanity can perfect itself. At dinner one evening he debates the Exhibition with Fleury and the Padre, arguing that the inventions it housed represent 'man's God-given ability to observe and calculate as minute steps in the progress of mankind towards union with that Supreme Being in whom all knowledge *is*, and ever shall be' (*SK* 53). But ideas are as much besieged in *The Siege of Krishapur* as the people who hold them. The siege forces a crisis in the Collector's views, and his gradual loss of faith leads him to seize and deploy with relish the Residency's objects to shore up the cantonment's ramparts and later as ammunition for the cannons. The recasting of the Residency's treasures creates many comic moments in the novel. They come to stand ironically as evidence of the fragility (rather than solidity) of colonial civilization and are revealed as complicit in the divisive and violent operations of colonial occupation.

Farrell's preferred word for such objects is 'possessions' (*SK* 93), which gathers together a number of important associations. It is a term which fuses that act of colonial occupation (India was a British 'possession'), the materiality of Empire and notions of being at the mercy of an external force which endangers one's sanity, as in 'being possessed'. The siege painfully forces the cantonment's British residents to confront dispossession: of Britain's authority in India, of the material comforts of expatriate life, and of the ideas they possess. Although the second of these is vividly portrayed in the novel, with the cantonment's residents gradually reduced to living in wretched conditions and resembling an 'extraordinary collection of scarecrows' (*SK* 307), it is the threatened dispossession of ideas which is the most painful to endure.

Farrell presents possession by ideas as a kind of dementia. As the siege worsens and circumstances change, several characters appear to lose their sanity in pursuit of the ideas they cling to with increasing volubility and ardour (we might recall Edward Spencer's similar activities in *Troubles*). A significant dispute breaks out between the cantonment's doctors, Dr Dunstable and Dr McNab, as to the correct way of being infected by and treating cholera. Dr McNab believes that cholera is caught through infected drinking water, while Dr Dunstable argues that it is spread in damp or impure air. Much comedy is made of this disagreement: several in the cantonment take to carrying cards which identify which doctor they wish to be treated by should they fall ill, and occasionally change the name on the card as the argument between the doctors swings back and forth (*SK* 253). But the debate takes a darker turn as Dr Dunstable becomes obsessive about his perceived rival's folly, slandering him in public. Eventually he is stricken by cholera, treated with saline injections by Dr McNab, and begins to recover. But on learning that he has been treated by 'that charlatan' (*SK* 270), he demands to be treated only with his own prescribed remedies for cholera. He declines again and dies of a heart attack.

The suggestion seems to be that those who cling blindly to their convictions are not only comical, but doomed. It is a point vividly made in relation to the Collector, who does succeed in relinquishing his convictions as the siege worsens. Near the end of the novel he is depicted seated on an oak throne which has one leg missing. As he realizes that the world of material progress means nothing without 'warmth of feeling. Without love', he is 'careful to embrace this conviction in a moderate manner, lest he be tipped out of the chair in which he was no longer sitting' (*SK* 301). The rampant, blinkered defence of one's convictions is presented as leading only to catastrophe.

Farrell's representation of India and Indians suggests a much greater self-consciousness of the limits of his novelistic vista, although problems remain concerning the depiction of the colonized which we encountered in *Troubles*. In his *Indian Diary*, a record of his 1971 visit to India, he remarks that:

> It's very easy to be a sahib in India, it seems. Servants are automatically deferential even to the most bizarre whims, which they seem to accept without surprise. Moreover, I wish my eye were better able to see the *differences* between them. I see things without understanding them. It took me ages to realize that what appeared to be splashes of blood all over the pavements of Bombay was merely people spitting betel juice. (*HS* 211)

Farrell confronts his British characters with a similar degree of restricted vision. Early in the novel Fleury comes across a shrine in the cantonment which stops him 'in his tracks' (*SK* 54). His bearer explains that it is a statue of Lord Bhairava:

> One of his six arms held a trident, another a sword, another flourished a severed forearm, a fourth held a bowl, while a fifth held a handful of skulls by the hair: the faces of the skulls wore thin moustaches and expressions of surprise. The sixth hand, empty, held up its three middle fingers. Peering closer, Fleury saw that people had left coins and food in the bowl he was holding and more food had been smeared around his chuckling lips, which were also daubed with crimson, as if with blood. Fleury turned away quickly, chilled by this unexpected encounter and anxious to leave this sinister garden without delay. (*SK* 55)

Fleury's response to this 'sinister' sight is, of course, displaced by the narrator. Fleury sees only the details of the shrine and cannot read its significance or function. But the bearer no doubt comprehends the significance of the shrine, and his presence registers the existence of native cultural and religious practices that silently challenges the authority of Fleury's response. The fact that the narrator places the bearer at the scene but never accesses his point of view might be seen by some as a blind spot in Farrell's writing. However, this is instead a moment of attempted sensitivity. Farrell takes the British in India to the very limits of their knowledge, rather than endorsing their perspectives. He acknowledges a way of seeing beyond Fleury's vision, but does not presume to be able to articulate differences which, as his *Indian Diary* suggests, he cannot fully understand. As the Collector comes to realize, 'there was a whole way of life of the people in India which he would never get to know and which was totally indifferent to him and his concerns' (*SK* 210). This is *not* a sign of the 'barbarism' of India, but a critical moment when the aggrandizement of nineteenth-century British colonialism is challenged and the boundaries of its vision are exposed.

That said, some complaints have been raised concerning Farrell's representation of the sepoys. As Farrell's friend and fellow-novelist Margaret Drabble puts it, 'the sepoys are never shown as people at all, but merely as cannon fodder' (*HS* 190), and there remains some legitimacy to this charge. Some awkwardness surrounds Farrell's depiction of the novel's Indian characters, especially the local Maharajah's son Hari. Hari is also a confirmed Anglophile and shares the Collector's love of possessions. We first see him sitting 'on a chair constructed entirely of antlers, eating a boiled egg and reading *Blackwood's Magazine*' (*SK* 70). He has received an English education and speaks a curious form of pidgin English, characterized by his constant misquoting of Shakespeare's plays. He is largely an unhappy character caught somewhere between Indian and British culture; a 'mimic man' whose attempt to copy the Collector's enthusiasm for innovation (Hari is obsessed with photography) makes him, in Homi Bhabha's terminology, 'Anglicised but emphatically not English [...] almost the same but not quite'.[10] Bhabha suggests that such figures, in general, menace the authority of the British colonizers by confronting them with a disconcerting image of resemblance which questions assumptions of the essential 'barbarity' of the colonized. However, Farrell's particular example of the 'mimic man' seems much less subversive and is, instead, an unhappy figure. His broken English and eccentricity mark him potentially as a buffoon. Frances B. Singh has also criticized Farrell for his delineation of Hari and the other Indian characters, arguing that their lack of stature is the novel's 'great tragedy'.[11] With the Prime Minister, Hari becomes imprisoned in the Residency as the siege worsens. When they are released, the Collector watches them leave the scene of the siege:

A little later from his bedroom, where he had retired for a rest, he watched through his daughters' brass telescope as the grey shadow of what once had been the sleek and lively Hari moved slowly over to the sepoy lines with, as usual, the Prime Minister dodging along behind him. (SK 211)

This is the last time these characters appear in the novel. They escape the limits of the novel's field of vision and we are not told where they go after their final exit.

While staying in a hotel in Agra in February 1971, Farrell noted that outside of the hotel's grounds lay 'the poverty and filth of the bazaar', while inside the hotel's dining room 'a bygone England prevails; a horde of waiters dressed up in elaborate cummerbunds and turbans' (HS 215). Farrell's writing was ultimately concerned with satirizing the latter of these worlds, the 'bygone' era of the British Raj. As he was well-aware, the region of the bazaar, and its Indian inhabitants, lay beyond his vista. None the less, in valuably acknowledging the limits of his vision Farrell's novel attempted to displace its version of the Mutiny from conventional colonialist representations. His strategic rewriting of history succeeded in building a comic yet critical view of the British in India at a time when few such novels existed. In terms of the Empire Trilogy, *The Siege of Krishapur* more purposefully attacks the ideology of Empire than the transitional *Troubles*. In particular, the increased attention to the materialism of Empire would become central concerns in Farrell's next novel, *The Singapore Grip*.

Farrell returned imaginatively to India in the novel he left unfinished at his death. Almost half of the novel (nineteen chapters) had been written as a first draft, while its remaining sections were summarized on a series of cards. It was posthumously published as *The Hill Station* in 1981. The title is not Farrell's but John Spurling's, who edited the typescript. Its setting is India in March 1871, specifically the Hill Station of Simla which was a temperate location popular with the British during the hot and dry months. It features two characters from *The Siege of Krishnapur*, Dr McNab and Miriam Dunstable, who have subsequently married. These circumstances immediately suggest a colonial theme, as in his first India novel, yet *The Hill Station* is much less directly concerned with the language and ideology of Empire.

The Hill Station concerns the visit of Dr and Miriam McNab to Simla in the company of their young niece, Emily Anderson, who has just arrived in India. On the long train journey to the hills they share a carriage with Reverend Kingston, the consumptive and emaciated curate of Saint Saviour's church in the Simla bazaar, and Mrs Forester who is travelling with her son, Jack. Once in Simla, Dr McNab learns that Kingston is unpopular as he has begun to alter his services to incorporate certain rituals (the lighting of candles, the burning of incense) which he regards as part of the church's proud traditions. These have angered the local Bishop and many of the clergy who feel that, through such actions, the Reverend may be surreptitiously converting them to Catholicism. The Bishop and other worried locals, such as Mr Lowrie, a prominent hotelier, are keen for Dr McNab to declare Kingston as unwell so that he can be removed from his post. McNab refuses to be drawn, although he is alarmed at Kingston's health and treats him privately. Things come to a head when, during one of Kingston's services, an angry crowd gathers outside the church to mock proceedings. A pig is let into the church, causing mayhem.

Meanwhile, Emily finds herself amorously pursued by several young officers, in particular Lieutenant Edward Potter, and the novel light-heartedly plots Potter's exuberant gallantry and Emily's coquettish responses. She also befriends Mrs Forester and is horrified to learn that she is regarded in society as a 'fallen' women due to an affair. Mrs Forester spends much of her time with Captain Hagan to the disapproval of Simla society. The sub-plot's characters are also present at the tumultuous scene at Saint Saviour's, where Mrs Forester and Captain Hagan are informed that Kingston will refuse to communicate them due to their sinful relationship. As far as Potter is concerned, their relationship has been misunderstood. As he tells Emily at the end of the abandoned service, 'It's the servants in India, Emily, they spread all sort of fanciful tales' (*HS* 151).

Exactly what happens next must remain a mystery, as these were the last lines of fiction Farrell wrote.[12] Although one must beware of making claims for a novel that was very much in its early stages of evolution, it seems the central dynamic of *The Hill Station* is an enquiry into faith. On the one hand, Farrell revisits late-nineteenth-century theological debates. He resurrects the arguments for and against ritualism in the Church of England, as part of a satirical representation of the edifying self-confidence of the previous century. Yet the novel's theological debate is also used as a way to ask more abstract questions about the pursuit of faith. On this point, Farrell returns to some of the preoccupations of the early novels, especially the relationship between the physical body and its spirit, soul or will, as well as continuing his fascination with those who pursue their convictions without moderation.

Farrell approaches these issues through the figure of Dr McNab. McNab's persona installs a temperate, self-questioning and wary consciousness at the heart of the novel which recalls the attitude of the Collector at the end of *The Siege of Krishnapur* sitting carefully on his three-legged throne. McNab's decades of medical experience, attempting to protect bodies from the fatal attack of disease, contribute to his composed, insular and melancholy persona. He stands in a long line of doctors in Farrell's fiction – one thinks of Dr Baker in *The Lung* and Dr Ryan in *Troubles* – but is the first to become a central character. He is the novel's interface between body and mind: a witness to the theological debate at large, and to Reverend Kingston's tuberculor illness. He is a confirmed sceptic, both in medical and spiritual matters. As he tells the Bishop, he believes in God 'In my own way' (*HS* 90) but tends towards doubt rather than creed and rarely attends church. Yet his experience of India has made him contemplate the power of faith, prompted by witnessing such sights as a Hindu holy man who has held his hand above his head for so long that 'it could no longer be lowered without surgery' (*HS* 112):

> And it seemed to McNab that if power of faith, of the spirit, or merely of the concentrated mind, could produce the least of these wonders in defiance of the physical world as the physician assumed it to be, then he would have to change his assumptions, or at least proceed with the utmost caution while he considered the matter. (*HS* 112)

McNab is intrigued by the relationship between mind and body and wonders if illness has a moral or social dimension. He is planning to write a treatise inspired by his feeling that 'all things were one, that everything was connected, that an illness was merely one of many fruits of an underground plant in the community as a whole. The illnesses popped up, here and there like mushrooms, apparently individual growths but all in fact the fruit of the same plant' (*HS* 73). More evidence of the 'moral dimension' (*HS* 80) to illness is provided to McNab when he witnesses the Bishop beat a much younger and fitter curate in an arm-wrestling challenge. McNab wonders if that 'physical strength is in some way connected with moral strength or strength of personality' (*HS* 80).

This is an issue which Farrell has explored before in his fiction, most notably in *The Lung* where Sands's survival from illness is as much a result of his fragile will as it is medical science in the shape of the iron lung. Although illness is never far away in Farrell's fiction, either literally or as metaphor, in *The Hill Station* it is particularly prominent. The novel opens with the hotelier, Mr Lowrie, ghoulishly contemplating the many invalids who travel to Simla to recuperate from their various illnesses, and amongst whom he has become skilled at predicting their chances of survival. McNab's niece, Emily, seems the picture of health, yet 'one of her arms hung rather loosely at her side and ended in a hand whose shrinking tendons had drawn its fingers into a permanently clutching little fist' (*HS* 17). Later on we learn of rumours of an outbreak of rabies in Simla. At times the novel recalls Thomas Mann's *Der Zauberberg* (1924) in its depiction of a small, isolated community beset by disease, and the contagious atmosphere of Camus's *La Peste* (1947) – two novels which Farrell particularly admired. At one point McNab admits to feeling uneasy in Simla 'as if beside the beautiful scenery, the prodigious vistas, the snow-capped mountains sparkling in the clean air, there lurked the malevolent presence of a disease he would be unable to control' (*HS* 113).

In this regard, Simla seems less important to Farrell as a material location and more significant as a metaphorical space or location of intellectual enquiry. The novel's characters are not undergoing a moment of historical crisis as they do in the Empire Trilogy. However, Ralph Crane and Jennifer Livett have suggested that the novel's setting in the 1870s is carefully chosen, late enough for memories of the Mutiny to have faded and prior to the growth of Indian Nationalist agitation in the 1890s.[13] It is an idyllic and relatively tranquil time for the British in India, perhaps, yet the novel sounds its death knell in its brief description of Karl Marx, sitting 'sucking a pencil' (*HS* 92) in the British Museum. 'Soon it will be closing time' (*HS* 92), he thinks, looking at the clock in the Reading Room. Marx's presence casts a dark shadow over the depiction of British colonial society in Simla: as Farrell knows, his writings will inspire a wealth of anti-colonial radicals throughout the colonized world who will effectively 'call time' on the rule of Empire.

Arguably, the two most important thinkers whose ideas would have a major impact on the fortunes of the twentieth century are Karl Marx and Sigmund Freud. Freud's work on psychoanalysis revolutionized the ways we regard the interface between body and mind. Dr McNab's enquiry into illness as having a social or moral dimension makes him seem, at times, something of an 'embryonic' Freudian. He is investigating issues similar to those Freud began to explore from the 1890s, although lacking a Freudian vocabulary with which to frame them (Freud would have been almost 15 years old in March 1871). In this regard, Reverend Kingston becomes a fascinating case study for McNab. Kingston's ardent pursuit of his faith stages the battle between body and soul which so intrigues McNab, and one wonders how he would have ultimately influenced the doctor's thinking about the moral aspect of illness had the novel been finished.

In *The Siege of Krishnapur* Kingston's steadfast pursuit of his Ritualism would have made him seem as crazed and absurd as Dr Dunstable or the Padre. However, in *The Hill Station* he is afforded much sympathy both through his illness and through Dr McNab's compassionate approach which eschews the malevolence of much of Simla's British population. His physical vulnerability humanizes him and makes his steadfast faith in his convictions seem courageous. In contrast, the Bishop seems a remote and authoritarian figure whose rude health contrasts starkly with the condition of his upstart curate. Considering McNab's instincts about the moral or social dimensions of illness, it is intriguing to contemplate the example given by Kingston's illness. Is it a result of Kingston's unwavering, intemperate pursuit of his beliefs – killing himself with the passion of his own convictions – which contrasts both with the Bishop's understated, unexcited authority and McNab's calm intelligence? Or might the illness be a physical manifestation of society's moral condemnation of his interpretation of the Church? It is interesting to learn that, according to Farrell's notes, Kingston was eventually to renounce his activities at the request of the Bishop who would appear to be dying. Whereas the Bishop would recover, Kingston would expire. Kingston's death would perhaps prove McNab's hunch that one's spirit could dictate the fortunes of the body, preserving or destroying it.

Although the world of *The Hill Station* seems much less urgently besieged than Kilnalough, Krishnapur or Singapore, the subtle Marxian and Freudian elements of the novel hint at the intellectual and political changes to come, as well as the debates of the next century which would succeed late-nineteenth-century anxieties of Ritualism. Although we are not allowed the pleasure of a dénouement, in the long term Simla and the society it represents are as doomed as Farrell's other colonial locations.

5

Singapore, 1937–1942

When *The Singapore Grip* was published in September 1978, a fledgling novelist called Timothy Mo had this to say about Farrell's longest and most ambitious novel to date:

> The novel may well be Farrell's private attempt at *War and Peace*. It is both a hilarious picture of the humanely ludicrous and an acute historical analysis, examining the old imperialism at its moment of dissolution in the Far East and considering the difficulties of behaving decently within that order.[1]

In dealing with events leading up to the fall of the colony of Singapore to Japanese forces in February 1942, Farrell addresses an historical affair which was, not only, one of Britain's greatest disasters of the Second World War but also signalled the beginning of the end of British colonial influence in South and East Asia. As befits such an experience, perhaps, Farrell's canvas is substantial: the novel runs to seventy-five chapters and ranges, in the manner of an epic film, over the fortunes of a sizeable cast of characters. In comparison with the other novels in the Empire Trilogy, *The Singapore Grip* describes a wider theatre of action: the cramped confines of the Majestic hotel or the cantonment at Krishnapur have expanded to embrace the city of Singapore, which gradually finds itself besieged by the Japanese forces, overwhelmed by refugees fleeing the hostilities in the Malayan peninsula, and, like the Majestic, is in flames by the end of the novel.

As one might expect, *The Singapore Grip* bears many of the hallmarks of Farrell's historical fiction: a besieged colonial community; the decline of colonial authority and understanding; an acerbic, comical rendering of those 'undergoing' history, bewildered by the changes which they struggle to command

and control. Yet in many ways *The Singapore Grip* is perhaps Farrell's most conventional historical novel. This is partly due, paradoxically, to the novel's ambitious scope. In contrast to his approach in *Troubles* and *The Siege of Krishnapur*, leading historical figures are not obliquely referenced but appear as important characters (such as Lieutenant General Arthur Percival, the British commander in the region), while the major historical incidents explored in the novel are not displaced from the primary theatre of action but impact directly upon the characters and the city. As well as visiting Singapore, Farrell meticulously researched *The Singapore Grip* in the British Library and the influence of his archival explorations are explicit throughout (he famously appended a bibliography to the novel of important documentary sources).

At times the novel may feel rather too weighed down by the burden of its scholarship, which occasionally works to constrain Farrell's imaginative adventurousness – to the extent that he sometimes writes more like a moonlighting historian than the ironical historical novelist of *Troubles*. Yet the novel's biggest challenge regards its negotiation between, in Mo's words, the 'hilarious picture of the humanely ludicrous and an acute historical analysis', which is not always successfully brokered. At times the historical and imagined worlds struggle to coalesce, meaning that Farrell's potentially most exciting and encyclopaedic novel remains a little flawed at its heart. Interestingly though, for all of its damning critique of the British Empire (perhaps the most vitriolic to be found in the Trilogy) it also articulates Farrell's most hopeful, utopian vision of human survival and progressive change.

The fall of the British colony of Singapore to the Japanese military in February 1942 was swift and dramatic. As well as an important military base, the island colony of Singapore and the Malayan mainland to the north had long been a significant commercial centre and a lucrative contributor to the fortunes of the British Empire – at one point almost half of the world's rubber and tin was manufactured in the region. Japanese imperial ambitions and military strength had been expanding from the early years of the twentieth century and were asserted aggressively in the 1930s; Singapore had become one of several locations (such as Hong Kong) in South East Asia which were attractive to imperial Japan for their economic and strategic military value. An attempt by the Japanese to occupy Singapore seemed increasingly likely in the 1930s, especially when the Second World War began in 1939. Yet a combination of bad judgement and complacency on the part of the British led many to believe that the colony could be easily defended – it was considered to be an impregnable fortress – and those in authority presumed Japan would probably pursue their imperial expansion elsewhere in the region. And as Lawrence James explains, a 'strong sense of racial superiority comforted everyone involved, including [the British Prime Minister] Churchill [...]; it was felt that [the Japanese] lacked the nerve, the wherewithal and the organisational skills to launch a successful invasion'.[2] History would prove otherwise.

In December 1941, Japanese forces launched a series of attacks on strategic targets in the vicinity (including Pearl Harbour, which brought the United States of America into the War), landing forces on the Malayan mainland on 8 December. These forces advanced steadily towards Singapore, meeting ineffective resistance from British and colonial forces, and quickly crossed into Singapore on 7 February 1942. The colony was surrendered to the Japanese on 15 February by General Percival and would remain under Japanese occupation until August 1945. From the perspective of the Empire, the fall of Singapore was one of the biggest humiliations of the Second World War.

In *The Singapore Grip* Farrell explores the fortunes, and the fall, of the British Empire squarely in terms of business, capital and wealth. The novel conceptualizes the Empire primarily as a vast money-making operation, one which made possible the creation of colossal riches for the British nation and those entrepreneurs whose businesses prospered through exploiting the commercial prospects of the colonies. It tells the story of the fictional company of Blackett and Webb, a key rubber producer in Singapore with considerable related business interests on the Malayan mainland. The firm is presided over by Walter Blackett, considered 'an important man in the Straits' (*SG* 16), who lives in the luxurious suburb of Tanglin with his wife Sylvia, two grown-up children, Joan and Monty, and his young daughter, Kate. His retired partner, the increasingly eccentric old Mr Webb, falls ill at a garden party hosted by Walter and his family in September 1940 and dies the following year. His death brings his son, Matthew Webb, to the colony on the eve of the Japanese invasion.

Matthew is young, idealistic and vocal in his criticism of the exploitative machinations of firms like Blackett and Webb. He soon develops an uneasy relationship with the Blacketts, particularly as he rebuffs Walter's attempts to secure the firm's future stability by facilitating a marriage of convenience between Matthew and the willing, odious Joan. As the novel proceeds, Farrell propels his characters through a number of uncomfortable experiences familiar to the preceding novels in the Trilogy. Like another Edward Spencer, Walter is forced to witness the security of his comfortable colonial environment fragment before his eyes and eventually be consumed by flames as the city burns; while Matthew finds his idealistic view of humanity tested to its very limits.

Farrell shapes several other characters whose stories add depth and complexity to the depiction of Singapore as it slides towards crisis and chaos. These include a Frenchman, François Dupigny, whose amused cynicism about human affairs comes to act as a bitter counterpoint to Matthew's seemingly inexhaustible optimism. On landing in Singapore, Matthew meets an old American friend, Ehrendorf, who pursues Joan amorously, and who formulates Ehrendorf's 'Second Law' which reflects starkly the doomed fortunes of colonial Singapore and many of its inhabitants: 'In human affairs, things tend inevitably to go wrong. Things are slightly worse at any given moment than at any preceding moment' (*SG* 295). Other old friends are present, especially for readers of the Trilogy: the Major, last seen in *Troubles*, reappears as a friend of old Mr Webb and the Blacketts, and, later, as an important member of the volunteer fire service (along with Matthew) struggling desperately to battle the flames as the Japanese attack Singapore. Farrell also takes us into the mind of Private Kikuchi, a Japanese soldier and part of the advance on the city, and Lieutenant General Percival, the British commander.

A particularly significant character is the 'Eurasian' Vera Chiang, allegedly the daughter of a Chinese man and a Russian aristocrat forced to flee to China after the Russian revolution. Befriended by old Mr Webb, she possesses a mysterious and dangerous past – Joan first meets her on a trip to Shanghai in 1937 when some Japanese soldiers attempt to seize her at the scene of a murder, and there are rumours of her connections with Chinese Communists. Matthew eventually develops a relationship with Vera and in the novel's last pages he attempts to secure her safe passage from Singapore, as the couple are terrified of what might happen to her when the Japanese eventually take control of the colony. Indeed, the novel's conclusion seems especially bleak: whereas the Blacketts and other members of the business community manage to escape just in time, Matthew, the Major and Dupigny are interred in Changi jail and later at the Sime Road civilian camp, presumably for the duration of the Second World War, and forced into a servile life of hard labour. As Lavinia Greacen has summarised, *The Singapore Grip* is characterized by a 'pervasive mood of despair' – although rather like *The Lung*, the novel's closing sentiments invite us movingly to reflect upon the faint possibility of hope and survival.[3]

Influenced by his reading of Marx and Engels and his extensive research into the operations of big business in South East Asia during the early twentieth century, Farrell's chief purpose in *The Singapore Grip* is to critique stridently the role of commerce and its centrality to British colonialism. In many ways Blackett and Webb stands not just for British commercial interests in the region at the time but also as a metaphor for the Empire as a whole: a large, web-like structure responsible for promoting Western business interests, destroying local economies and creating unfair conditions for colonized working people, who are held securely in the grip of an avaricious form of authority that cares little for their rights. The guise of colonial society, with its seeming orderliness, affluence and cultured ascendancy, is dependent upon, and creates, levels of poverty, inequality and exploitation not often acknowledged when the story of colonial expansion is proudly related.

It is significant that the novel begins by depicting the 'quiet and orderly' (*SG* 12) suburb of Tanglin where the Blacketts live in their magnificent house on Orchard Road, before following the road's gentle downward slope for a mile or so into Chinatown and the city's sordid commercial quarters, inhabited by 'the densely packed native masses' (*SG* 12). As the narrator remarks:

Imagine a clock in a glass case; the hands move unruffled about their business, but at the same time we can see the workings of springs and wheels and cogs. That ordered life in Tanglin depended on the same way in the city below, and on the mainland beyond the Causeway, whose trading, mining and plantation concerns might represent wheels and cogs while their mute, gigantic labour force are the springs, steadily causing pressures to be transmitted from one part of the organism to another (*SG* 12)

When Walter takes one of Joan's young suitors for a tour of his house early in the novel, he is keen to celebrate the beneficial face of colonial business in Singapore by pointing out a number of paintings which depict the transformation of Rangoon from a 'sleepy little village' into 'a great modern city' (*SG* 17). The paintings depict the British ships, the growing harbour, the new factories and warehouses. Walter's commentary celebrates the ingenuity of entrepreneurs and the achievements of modern engineering, such as the opening of the Suez Canal which enabled the shipping of cleaned rice to Europe, hence cutting out the need for fine-millers who cleaned the 'cargo rice' when it reached places such as London. What is missing, of course, from Walter's history lesson is an acknowledgement of precisely the wheels and cogs of industry that depend upon the poorly-rewarded toil of the 'mute labour force' and the mean conditions under which they labour. Much of *The Singapore Grip* is concerned with challenging Walter's proud version of the beneficial effects of the business of Empire. This is done, primarily, by mocking the ways in which commerce is celebrated by Walter and his ilk and, occasionally, by fore-grounding the squalid lives of those who have been muted by Walter's imperious history. As Paul Smethurst argues, the novel 'is about the processes and representation of history as much as the particular history it reports'.[4] As in the previous Trilogy novels, Farrell exposes and challenges the ways in which the Empire represents itself, subverting the prevailing symbolic and linguistic resources that buttressed the pursuit of wealth in 1940s Singapore.

Walter Blackett, cheerful patriarch and ruthless businessman, is perhaps the least likeable of Farrell's colonials. Like Edward Spencer and the Collector he possesses a bizarre animal-like appearance, but the effect is much more sinister and feral rather than humorous. Whereas these other characters appear comically, almost affectionately leonine at times, Walter possesses a menacing ridge of thick hairs which grow along the line of his vertebrae and which rise when he is either angry or sexually aroused: 'His wife had once confided in him that every night of their honeymoon she had been visited by a dream in which she had been led by a boar into the depths of a forest; there on a carpet of leaves, marooned in loneliness, she had been mounted by the animal in the grunting silence of the trees' (*SG* 40). As we shall soon see, elsewhere in the novel Farrell develops a portrayal of commerce in disturbingly sexual terms, which is suggested here in the unpalatable image of the businessman as rutting boar. The tempered sympathy extended to Edward Spencer's emotional disintegration in *Troubles* is withheld from Walter, and he never comes to question his deeply-held values as does the Collector in *The Siege of Krishnapur* – rather, his confidence in his views remains to the end, despite the fact that as Singapore burns he loses his 'grip on reality' (*SG* 436).

Walter's endeavour to secure the future of Blackett and Webb by finding a suitor for Joan, and hence arranging a marriage of convenience purely in the interests of business, reveals the extent to which his pursuit of commercial superiority over-rides more humane concerns, even when conditions in besieged Singapore become desperate. Once Matthew has rejected the scheme to be married to Joan, Walter attempts to get her betrothed to the son of his greatest competitor, Solomon Langfield, much to his competitor's amusement. He even lies to Langfield's son about his father's views of such a match not long after Langfield's death. Walter cares little for Matthew's increasingly desperate requests to help Vera leave Singapore safely. Nothing really matters to him except the safety of his business empire.

Joan's willingness to marry Matthew for business interests underlines the perverting primacy of commercial values in the Blackett household. As Matthew lies in bed recuperating from a fever not long after arriving in Singapore, he is visited by Walter, Joan and the Major. Drenched by a fall of rain, Joan removes her dress as Matthew and the Major watch embarrassedly and gets into bed with Matthew: 'Walter beamed at Matthew more expansively than ever. "Well, there you are, my boy", he seemed to be saying. "There are the goods. You won't find better. You can see for yourself. It's a good offer. Take it or leave it'" (*SG* 262). As well as demonstrating how much the language of business has come, perversely, to shape human relations, this incident positions Walter and Joan almost as pimp and prostitute, using the business of pleasure to generate and secure financial gain. Throughout the novel Farrell is at pains to represent the pursuit of business as creating exploitative human relationships analogous to those forged between client and whore, and in so doing he offers perhaps his most coruscating critique of the machinations of Empire throughout the Trilogy.

The connection between industry and prostitution is clinched in the novel's title, the meaning of which remains a mystery to Matthew for much of the novel. He eventually learns from Ehrendorf that it refers to the talents of the city's whores, 'the ability acquired by certain ladies of Singapore to control their autonomous vaginal muscles, apparently with delightful results' (*SG* 498). Matthew quickly offers his own rendering of the phrase: 'It's the grip of our Western culture and economy on the Far East... It's the stranglehold of capital on the traditional cultures of Malaya, China, Burma, Java, Indo-China and even India herself!' (*SG* 498). A stirring example of this connection is also given earlier in the novel when Monty, Walter's son, tries to convince Matthew to buy a share in a prostitute whom he and his friends want to maintain (Matthew declines) and, later, takes him for a night out to a brothel in Chinatown. The incident underlines Matthew's naïvety and innocence, but is most memorable for its sobering description of the Chinese prostitutes who are paraded before Monty and Matthew. One of them, a young girl with pigtails, is endeavouring to finish her homework:

> The young Chinese girl, having finished her Latin as best she could, had turned to arithmetic. Now she was sitting, stark naked, sucking her pencil over a problem which involved the rate at which a tap filled a bath. What, she wondered, was a tap? And what, come to that, was a bath? She would have to consult her aunt who was one of the older women with scarlet cheekbones. (*SG* 195)

The grip of 'Western culture and economy' upon the unnamed girl seems almost total. Her study of an incomprehensible (and dead) foreign language, as well as the puzzle concerning the bath, point to the power of Western forms of knowledge and cultural practices. Her labour as a prostitute exposes the economic superiority of Westerners in Singapore, one which has damaged local cultural and economic practices and forced this girl to consider exchanging sexual favours for money by labouring as a whore. It is no surprise, perhaps, that she feels that 'an invisible net had been thrown over her and that an unseen hand was beginning to pull the cords tight' (*SG* 195). Caught in the web of Singapore's commercial and cultural colonisation, the girl's subaltern existence is both the product and the shame of Empire.

For Farrell, the exploitation of these women is of a kind with the exploitation of the rubber workers and other labourers caught in the grip of Empire. It is significant that Matthew is also taken, this time by Vera, to a 'dying-house' in Chinatown where he is confronted by the wrecked bodies of those who have broken themselves working on the plantations and in the factories but cannot afford healthcare. Those he finds there confront him with evidence of cruelty and exploitation by businesses including Blackett and Webb and castigate the rubber industry as a 'bloody big swindle' (*SG* 346). In depicting the decrepit workers confronting Matthew to harangue him for his connections to Blackett and Webb – 'supine figures were sitting up and casting off their shrouds and bandages, while others were clambering down from the tiers of shelves on which they had been stretched' (*SG* 347) – Farrell attempts to bear witness to, and briefly break the silence of, the vast mute workforce whose experience of industry would surely challenge Walter's proud version of events supported by his collection of paintings. In so doing, *The Singapore Grip* perhaps goes further than the previous novels in trying to articulate the position of subaltern figures, albeit briefly, and to direct attention to their absence from received history.

It is significant that the narration of the first Japanese air-raid on Singapore in January 1942 closes with the destruction of the cramped tenement buildings in Chinatown. An elderly 'wharf-coolie' rises from his cubicle to visit the toilet outside in the yard and is killed when the building is bombed. 'Later', we are told 'when official estimates are made of this first raid on Singapore (sixty-one killed, one hundred and thirty-three injured), there will be no mention of this old man for the simple reason that he, in common with so many others, has left no trace of ever having existed either in this part of the world or in any other' (*SG* 218). At moments such as these, Farrell's writing is at its most postcolonial in its determined attempt to bear witness to, and count the cost, of the lives of those deemed unworthy of historical witness.

Farrell's attention to the obscenity of Empire, mediated through a palpable if tightly disciplined sense of outrage, makes for sobering reading. But as one might expect, *The Singapore Grip* also mobilizes a more comical register typical of the Empire Trilogy as a whole. As in his previous work, Farrell's critique of the Empire deploys comical elements which satirize and deflate colonial modes of representation. These elements can be discerned in the narrative of Walter's attempt to celebrate the fiftieth anniversary of his company's presence in the colony with 'one of those monster carnival parades so beloved of the Chinese in Singapore' (*SG* 34). The parade affords Farrell a characteristic opportunity to play mischievously with the symbolic resources of Empire and oppose Walter's imperial bombast by creating deflating laughter. Walter often represents his enthusiasm for the parade to the Major, who is reluctantly cajoled into participating in rehearsals. For Walter, the parade 'deals in symbols' (*SG* 43) and is intended 'not only [as] a patriotic cavalcade of a magnificence rarely seen, it would also be a living diagram, as it were, of the Colony's economy in miniature' (*SG* 249).

It is planned to consist of a series of floats, with allegorical names such as Continuity and Prosperity, each of which dramatizes a particular aspect of the beneficial consequences of British business interests in Singapore. One float features Joan, dressed in a white robe of Grecian appearance, holding a trident and a Britannic shield. Accompanying the floats will be a counter-parade that highlights the many obstructions to business which Blackett and Webb has successfully overcome, made up of 'Chinese acrobats, schoolboys, and volunteers of all races' (*SG* 249) dressed as imps and devils representing 'Labour Unrest', 'Rice Hoarding' and 'Wage Demands'. These figures will run alongside the main floats prodding them with pitchforks and playfully antagonizing the crowd (during one rehearsal the Major appears looking extremely uncomfortable in a devil's suit, complete with horns).

Walter's obsession with putting on the parade, despite Singapore's increasingly besieged condition, soon becomes a marker of his detachment from the colony's grim reality, while in rehearsals the parade itself ironically comes to suggest exactly the opposite of what is intended. The counter-parade hints at the disruption, conflict and inequalities created by commerce – as the attention to wage unrest shows, the prosperity created by business has not been made available to all. Rather than upholding the gravitas and pomposity of imperial grandeur, the parade also unleashes a carnivalesque critique of Empire in the Bakhtinian sense, as Walter's symbols of commerce and colonialism find themselves unintentionally transformed into delightfully bawdy yet telling figures of colonial exploitation.[5] Walter is incensed to discover that Monty has interfered with one of the floats on which his young sister, Kate, sits holding a sumptuous cornucopia of rubber products, such as rubber-tipped pencils, balloons and elastic bands:

> To this magnificent array Monty, as a joke, had attempted to add a packet of contraceptives. As ill luck would have it, Walter had noticed his son chuckling gleefully as he arranged something conspicuously on the very lip of the cornucopia. His display of anger, even to Monty who was accustomed to it, had been frightening. (SG 355)

The contraceptives hint at the link made elsewhere between commerce and sexual contact, and ground the loftiness of the parade in a smutty world of sex with which Monty seems obsessed throughout the novel.

Another carnivalesque travesty of the parade happens to a float featuring a symbolic rubber tree which pours liquid gold into a basin. The free-flowing liquid gold is intended to signify the wealth and prosperity created by the rubber industry, but a rather different effect is inadvertently created:

> 'It looks as if it's ... well ...' said the Major.
> 'Yes I'm afraid it does rather [replied Walter]. But it was the best we could do. At first we tried a little conveyer belt inside the trunk which kept spilling coins through the opening in the bark and that looked fine, but the blighters kept pinching the coins.' (SG 361)

It is a deliciously comic and ironic moment. The fact that masquerading children steal from a display which is meant to symbolize the beneficial prosperity of the Empire underlines the divisions of wealth in the colony, while the image of the urinating tree delightfully travesties the lofty symbolism of Empire and recasts an image of affluence as a bizarre sign of excrescence. As in the previous novels, representations of colonial propriety and confidence are made to malfunction as Farrell engages comically yet critically with colonial discourses of grandeur.

The Singapore Grip contains several characters who offer a sceptical view of colonialism, the most significant of whom is Matthew Webb. As a young man Matthew worked for a charitable organisation called Committee for International Understanding which lobbied the League of Nations in 1930s Geneva. He arrives in Singapore brimming with idealistic notions of international co-operation and universal suffrage which, not surprisingly, make him passionately opposed to colonialism. As he tells Monty during their first encounter, he is profoundly interested 'in political strikes and the relations of native workers to European employers', indeed 'the "colonial experience" as a whole' (*SG* 107). Matthew spends large parts of the novel arguing fervently over the injustices of colonialism with just about anyone who will listen. When he accompanies Monty to the Chinatown brothel – he has no idea where he is being taken and seems oblivious to his surroundings when he is there – he spends almost the entire encounter lecturing Monty on the failures of the League of Nations over its handling of the Manchurian Incident of 1931, before falling into a fever. Indeed, there is something oddly feverish about Matthew's obsessive attempt to argue the toss with all and sundry: at times his speeches resemble extracts from history books and, considering their fine detail and tone of certainty, may test the patience of the reader of a novel.

It must be said that several of the other characters, such as General Percival, also muse at length on historical circumstances in a mode which seems more suitable to an historical rather than a fictional text; and while this may be a sign of *The Singapore Grip*'s playful commingling (or dissolving) of the genres of history and fiction, it might also suggest that Farrell at times struggles to craft a novel which, remembering Timothy Mo's words, harmoniously facilitates a 'hilarious picture of the humanely ludicrous' and 'acute historical analysis'.

In Matthew, Farrell creates a naïve, ardent and idealistic central figure not simply as a convenient mouthpiece for anti-colonial sentiment, but more thoughtfully as the means to appraise the methods and agency of anti-colonial thought. In so doing, Farrell self-consciously investigates the challenges to and limits of the opposition to Empire, suggesting that escaping and opposing the grip of colonialism is a remarkably difficult task (one which, of course, the Empire Trilogy is also attempting to pursue). Matthew is happy to espouse his theories of the evils of colonialism and the possibilities of international co-operation, but what power do they have to establish lasting material change? Through the sympathetic figure of Matthew, Farrell asks questions about the effectiveness of oppositional thought, and questions its proximity to those who have suffered the most when undergoing the history of Empire. How can the world of ideas and idealism, of critical intention and utopian imagining – also the world of the novel, of course – assist and resource the 'mute, gigantic labour force' of Singapore, or the Indian sepoys or Catholic Irish? It is not enough merely to espouse doctrine, perhaps.

As we saw in the Introduction, Farrell had caused a stir in the media in 1973 when, during his acceptance speech for that year's Booker Prize, he criticised Booker McConnell's treatment of low-paid workers in the Far East and declared that he would use his prize-money (£5000) to write 'a full-scale study of commercial exploitation, set around the fall of Singapore in 1941'.[6] And while the resulting novel is unequivocal evidence of Farrell's serious commitment to challenge capitalism and colonialism, the figure of Matthew maybe captures something of Farrell's unease with the capability of the imagination to contest the world in general, as well as his particular sense of uncomfortable complicity in the affluent West.

It is worth noting that Matthew's trip to the 'dying-house' is a troubling experience for him. Surrounded by sobering evidence of the human cost of colonialism – one of the ex-workers makes him read a newspaper article from *The Planter* condemning the rubber industry – Matthew appears much more disconcerted than inspired, and there is something unhappy about the way he 'looked down at his watch as they [the ex-workers] crowded round him' (*SG* 347). He is happy to pronounce judgement on the world's problems and voice his solidarity with the wretched of the earth from the abstracting distance of Geneva, perhaps, but he strikes a different pose when faced with the realities of commerce in Malaya – and, let us not forget that, as a son of the former senior partner, his Oxford education and relatively affluent lifestyle in Geneva have been funded by the very industry which the ex-workers condemn.

Matthew's arguments often fall upon deaf ears or are met with a scornful cynicism by those who, equally, might not share an enthusiasm for colonialism. Few are interested in his condemnatory exposure of Empire's exploitative practices, while his idealistic faith in universal brotherhood is received rather pityingly. In one engagement with Dupigny, Matthew challenges the view that people are motivated by self-interest by declaring that 'I'm sure you'll find, once this dreadful war is over, that thousands of people of different races have been willing to risk their lives for each other' (*SG* 333). Dupigny responds, famously, by saying with a laugh: 'You might just as well expect stockbrokers to be ready to die for the Stock Exchange' (*SG* 333). For all of its sympathy with Matthew's politics, the novel tends to uphold Dupigny's dispiriting view of human affairs. In the closing pages, Matthew and Vera's attempt to escape Singapore on a boat is thwarted when a group of ragged Australian soldiers seize it at gunpoint and shoot Dupigny in the leg. So much for universal brotherhood. As well as upholding the dispiriting sense that events in the novel seem to prove Ehrendorf's Second Law – things are always getting worse, never better – the novel suggests that humanity is an ailing, cynical thing, unworthy of celebration. This view is wittily epitomized by an abandoned dog which is left in the care of the Major. Rancid and decrepit, the dog is an elderly 'King Charles spaniel: its coat, which had plainly come under attack from some worm, was in some patches bald, in others matted and filthy; its tail hung out at a drunken angle and was liberally coated in some dark and viscous substance resembling axle grease' (*SG* 247). With a darkly Beckettian humour, Dupigny christens the 'diminutive, elderly and frail' (*SG* 267) dog as The Human Condition.

None the less, while *The Singapore Grip* may well be despairing of the human condition it is not devoid of hope. Farrell is keen to problematize Matthew's glib confidence in universal brotherhood and benign humanity, to be sure, but at the same time he determinedly attempts to retain faith with the spirit of Matthew's views, not least because they incubate hope for a postcolonial future. Just as in *The Lung*, the relentless juggernaut of misery, despair and melancholy is not allowed entirely to vanquish the faint yet persistent pulse of endurance and – most importantly – survival: it is significant that The Human Condition is last spied escaping Singapore on a ship. Matthew never accedes to Dupigny's dismal pessimism, and by the end of the novel there is something admirable in his desire to cling to an optimistic view of humanity, especially after he has experienced humanity at its worse, at war. By the end of the novel, when he is interned, his naïve, abstract view of life has been replaced by bitter experience and, sadly, '[h]ope had deserted him completely' (*SG* 565). He still attempts to defend his former views to Dupigny, but he lacks certainty and conviction. Yet, during the second year of his captivity, while he is out with a working party on the road, a young Chinese presses a cigarette packet into his hand:

> When he opened it he put his head in his hands: it contained a lump of sugar and two cooked white mice. And he thought: 'Well, who knows? At least there's a chance. Perhaps she'll survive after all, and so will I.' (*SG* 566)

The 'she' referred to here is Vera Chiang, and the incident (which comes almost at the novel's end) refers us back to two of its key related elements: the relationship between Matthew and Vera, and The Great World fair where the couple meet and which, along with the Tanglin suburb and Chinatown, is the third major location in Farrell's Singapore. As well as being one of the more successful romantic relationships in Farrell's *œuvre*, Matthew's affair with Vera sets him on a passage from innocence to experience, both in terms of sexual experience but also (as I suggested above) first-hand knowledge of the unhappy conditions of Singapore's poor.

A refugee from the political upheavals of Russia and later China, it is intimated that Vera has worked as a prostitute in 1930s

Shanghai, and hence she is linked to the novel's wider rendering of colonial disenfranchisement in terms of sexual exploitation. But she is primarily a survivor and possesses the ability to resist the power of Empire to determine her life. Indeed, her caring and sensuous nature offers an alternative representation of sexuality in the novel which reaches far beyond the gross contractual personal encounters that are elsewhere emphasized. And while some readers may feel that as a sensuous 'Eurasian' woman Vera's character is a benign-looking example of the female exotic quite common in colonialist representations of Eastern women, it must be said that she is portrayed with well-intentioned sensitivity and is much more carefully imagined than Hari in *The Siege of Krishnapur*.

The reference to white mice in the previous quotation reminds Matthew of a meal he enjoyed with Vera in her cramped cubicle in a Chinatown tenement, where he sampled 'white mice, poached Chinese-style' (*SG* 410). His stay with Vera in the tenement exposes him to the bleak circumstances of Singapore's poor – from the street outside he hears 'the very rhythm of poverty and despair, [a] weary, tubercular coughing which never ceased' (*SG* 411) – but also to the possibilities of human contact; of love, sensuality and warmth. Matthew and Vera's tender relationship appears almost as a private, domestic version of the possibilities which Matthew hopes for in the world of public, international affairs created out of the benevolent encounters between people of different cultures and locations.

The epitome of this humane spirit is arguably The Great World fair, where Vera and Matthew first meet, which offers an alternative, festive vision of the hope for human encounters far beyond the cynical contractual modes of Empire. The sensual atmosphere of the fair is caught memorably in Farrell's description of its effect on Matthew: 'That atmosphere of cigar smoke and sandalwood, incense and perfume, that stirring compound of food and dust and citrus bloom, of sensuality and spices filled Matthew with such excitement that his spirit began flapping violently inside him like a freshly caught fish in a basket' (*SG* 386). Bringing together and commingling the different cultural influences of Europe and Asia, The Great World is a luxurious space of (re)creation and liberty which exists beyond the illiberal propriety and protocols of race and nation. The symbolic resources of Empire do not work here. In one comic incident, Matthew watches a side-show in which a Miss Kennedy-Walsh, BA (Pass Arts), H Dip Ed, TCD, is to be fired from a cannon at a model of an armoured car featuring the head of the Japanese Emperor Hirohito. This attempt to portray the Empire's superiority over its imperial rival, Japan, is delightfully travestied when, first, the cannon fails to fire, and second, when Miss Kennedy-Walsh misses the car entirely. Matthew is lost momentarily amongst the human traffic of the fair, which consists of those 'of every shape, size and colour, from a family of performing pygmies, to the graceful, delicate Chinese, to floury, bucolic British and Dutch in voluminous khaki shorts' (SG 163). He is struck by a momentary vision of Singapore's possible postcolonial future, created out of the very diversity brought by (and disruptive of) the interests of Empire, as he watches a crowded dance-floor featuring:

> that bewildering array of races and types he had noticed earlier in the evening in the open air, even two members of the family of pygmies could be seen executing a perfect tango close at hand. Matthew gazed enchanted at the teeming dance-floor. Abruptly, he realised why this sight gave him such pleasure. He tried to explain to Monty who had taken Joan's place at his side: *this was the way Geneva should have been*! Instead of that grim segregation by nationality they should have all spent their evenings like this, dancing the tango or the quick-step or the *ronggeng* or whatever it was with each other: Italians with Abyssinians, British with Japanese, Germans with Frenchmen and so on. [...] 'It was [said Matthew] the feeling, perhaps even the *confidence* that men of different nations and races could get on together that was so tragically missing. And yet here is the evidence! Men are brothers!' (SG 181–2)

In contrast to Edward Spencer's ball in *Troubles*, which tries to resurrect a vanishing milieu, Matthew regards the dance as a forward-looking, potentially progressive image of a world transformed, with old conflicts and divisions duly resolved. It may be tempting to regard Matthew's vision as more evidence of his naïve idealism, and the novel certainly shows how national aggression and segregation may triumph. Yet the *confidence* that the world might be changed by the coming together of diverse peoples remains until the novel's conclusion, even if such change did not happen in Malaya in the 1930s and

1940s; this is why, perhaps, Matthew receives the white mice near the end of the novel as they embody the surviving spirit and utopian potential of The Great World.

The Singapore Grip maintains the transformative, creative potential of this festive environment to the end, while remaining alert, through the character of Matthew, to its tendency towards glib idealism and romanticization. Despite its prevailing atmosphere of despair, the novel's determined confidence in the capacity for change makes it perhaps the most hopeful of the Empire Trilogy, much as *The Lung* strikes the most affirmative note of the predominantly bleak early novels. The closing chapter of *The Singapore Grip* exemplifies its character in this regard. Set in 1976 it depicts Kate Blackett, now fully grown, relaxing with her companion, whom the narrator hints is a grey-haired Ehrendorf. The companion reads Kate an article from the *The Times* of 10 December 1976 – written, wittily, by 'Our Correspondent, Geneva' (*SG* 567) – describing the meagre conditions of plantation workers. The incident invites us to reflect on the possibility of change. Recalling Malaya as a distant, unreal place, Kate considers that 'Things that once seemed immutable have turned out to be remarkably vulnerable to change' (*SG* 567).

Her companion is less certain, and wonders if the article proves that 'nothing very much had changed, after all, despite that tremendous upheaval in the Far East?' (*SG* 567). *The Singapore Grip* closes by keeping open the debate which the Empire Trilogy has conducted across three memorable and striking novels. And although the book, if not the Trilogy as a whole, often despairingly posits a gloomy vision of human life as one of irreversible degeneration and decay, as summed up by Ehrendorf's Second Law, Ehrendorf's seeming survival (like the Major's recuperation in *Troubles*, perhaps) stops this vision from establishing itself as conclusive and indeed suggests an alternative vista of human endurance and perseverance. To borrow from the novel's closing words, 'Tomorrow is another day, as they say, as they say' (*SG* 568), and it can never be truly predicted what changes tomorrow might bring. For Farrell, life may at times seem a journey towards inevitable disintegration and collapse; but still, perhaps, there are always the hopes and possibilities, however slender, of tomorrow.

6

Critical Legacy

'It is evident that *The Singapore Grip* relates naturally by theme and method to *Troubles* and *The Siege of Krishnapur* and that taken together these three novels form a major contribution to recent English fiction, and an important addition to the literature of imperialism.'[1] So wrote Bernard Bergonzi in 1979, in the final paragraph of the second edition of *The Situation of the Novel*. These words, written while Farrell was alive, are both accurate and misleading, and point to some of the problems that have arisen when critics have approached Farrell's work, especially in the decade immediately after his untimely death. On the one hand, Farrell's prominent place in Bergonzi's chapter 'Fictions of History' rightly positions Farrell as a significant novelist deserving of attention and praise. Yet Bergonzi's view was by no means widespread and in many ways is exceptional to, rather than typical of, recent accounts of postwar fiction. As John Banville has pointed out, '[Farrell's] death at forty-four, a tragically early age, led to an inexplicable decline in his reputation'.[2] The consequences are notable: Farrell's work is given only cursory attention in Malcolm Bradbury's *The Modern British Novel* (1993), Steven Connor's *The English Novel in History 1950–1995* (1995), D. J. Taylor's *After the War* (1993), and Patricia Waugh's *Harvest of the Sixties* (1995). As we shall see very briefly, it is indeed possible to explain the decline in Farrell's critical fortunes which, happily, have today well and truly revived.

One important reason concerns the fact that Farrell's mature work engaged with Empire and the consciousness of (mostly) British colonials. At first several critics struggled to understand the particular kind of representation of Empire which Farrell attempted. Bergonzi's phrase 'the literature of imperialism' lacks precision as a description of the Empire Trilogy and points to the ways in which some have failed to comprehend Farrell's writing. In much criticism of the 1980s Farrell found himself increasingly linked to a tradition of writing about Empire which was waning: he was seen very much as a writer who not only wrote about endings – of colonialism, authority, power – but was also at the end of a well-worn literary practice that (happily, for some) was in its closing stages. Consequently, he has often been passed over by critics either unable or unwilling to engage sensitively with the form and focus of his work. Only in the 1990s did a new critical approach to Farrell emerge which saw beyond the blinkered perspectives that hindered earlier responses to his work and challenged the prevailing orthodoxy. As a result of recent critical endeavours, by the beginning of the twenty-first century, Farrell's work has gained not only proper recognition, but also is much better understood.

Bergonzi's was perhaps the most sensitive and thoughtful of the early critical approaches to Farrell's work. Recognizing the surreal aspects of Farrell's writing and his ironic manipulation of literary conventions, Bergonzi argues that Farrell had not so much abandoned realism as a literary mode but 'rethought its possibilities'.[3] His writing, it was claimed, was in dialogue with novelistic convention, and might best be described as 'conscious realism' – a mode which offered a way out of the impasse many writers felt between conventional and experimental fictional styles.[4] Yet several critics did not share Bergonzi's sensitivity to Farrell's technique, his artful combination of realism with more absurdist elements. In a period where the experimental novel was very much in vogue due to the work of John Fowles, B. S. Johnson, Thomas Pynchon and others, to many Farrell's novels seemed too ordinary, lacking in explicit innovation and formal experimentation. For a while this led to Farrell's work being either praised for its obedience to conventionality or dismissed for its alleged formal unadventurousness.

Neil McEwan, an early enthusiast, claimed in 1987 that Farrell 'accepts the older conventions of modern prose narrative and believes they reflect what we normally experience. [...] Farrell is a realist.'[5] In seeking to appropriate Farrell as part of a spirited contestation of experimental fiction, McEwan overlooked those elements of Farrell's style which disturbed realism, and also ignored Farrell's Irish connections in declaring him a British writer. From another perspective, in the same year as McEwan's work appeared, the esteemed critic Malcolm Bradbury witheringly dismissed the Empire Trilogy as unambitious for succumbing to the 'gravitational tug of realism' from which so much contemporary writing had broken free (although he would come to modify his thoughts in the following decade).[6] Farrell's writing was often mistaken for conventional realism at a time when realism had become almost a derogatory term for many scholars of literary fiction, and his reputation suffered accordingly.

If Farrell, apparently, was working in a literary tradition that looked backwards rather than forwards, his reputation was also tarnished as a consequence of his subject matter, the end of the British Empire. Bergonzi's phrase 'the literature of Imperialism' points to the difficulties many critics faced when locating Farrell's major work. Farrell was writing about the end of colonialism and contesting its attitudes and arrogance, and he had much in common with many Commonwealth writers – Ngugi wa Thiong'o, Patrick White, Anita Desai – who were also exploring similar themes at the time. Yet writing, and writers, from Ireland were never considered part of Commonwealth literature (not least because Ireland left the Commonwealth in 1948), so an attempt to think about Farrell comparatively in terms of such writers did not immediately emerge. Many did not see the ways in which Farrell opened a critical vision of colonialism even if he did not write squarely from the perspective of the (formally) colonized.

As Ralph Crane and Jennifer Livett explain, Farrell primarily wrote about the effect of colonization on the colonizing power itself, but in the critical climate of the time 'this approach [to Empire] looked misguided if it was recognised at all'.[7] Consequently, Farrell's work was annexed instead to a tradition of British writing about Empire summed up in Bergonzi's phrase; a tradition which, by the early 1980s, had come to be regarded often derogatively as nostalgic for lost imperial glories. A typical example can be found in Randall Stevenson's *The British Novel Since the Thirties* (1986), where Farrell appears alongside Paul Scott, author of the *Raj Quartet* (1966-74), in a chapter titled 'Lost Empires'.[8] Patricia Waugh persisted with this attitude when she argued that the novels of Scott and Farrell 'though innovatory, remained broadly within the Eurocentric paradigm, challenging but remaining situated within the consciousness of the British characters. This tendency of earlier fictions of empire was questioned in the 1980s by the literary attention given to the problems of post-colonial peoples'.[9]

Damned as a realist and dismissed as a British colonial nostalgic, Farrell's work was deemed unfashionable and outmoded. When a new generation of postcolonial novelists emerged in the 1980s – Salman Rushdie, Timothy Mo, Caryl Phillips – whose writing looked critically and playfully at the legacy of colonialism, at first Farrell's work was rarely mentioned in this company, nor was it seen as inspiring many of these figures who would soon establish themselves as major writers. Ironically, postcolonial literary studies would play an important role in re-evaluating Farrell's representation of Empire in the following decade.

Notwithstanding the prevailing critical vogue of the time, there appeared insightful responses to Farrell in the 1980s which offered more sensitive approaches to his work, although they were few and far between. As Crane and Livett remark, '[Ronald] Binns and the authors of a handful of book chapters and journal articles on Farrell remained fairly lonely voices until the early 1990s'.[10] Binns's important single-volume study of 1986, *J. G. Farrell*, did much to maintain Farrell's critical standing and stopped his work from being obscured by the inappropriate categories quickly applied by others. Binns's book is attentive to Farrell's complex background between Britain and Ireland and demonstrates the eschewal of the conventional English novel in the Empire Trilogy. In particular, Binns shows how Farrell's mature writing, ironic and melancholy, was always endeavouring to critique the purpose and grandiosity of colonialist attitudes, while opening up more philosophical perspectives concerning the often tragic condition of human existence. He also offers an important short appraisal of the early novels. The clarity, intelligence and admirable sensitivity of Binns's study means that it remains a valuable, informative resource for Farrell scholars twenty years after its publication.

There are several reasons why Farrell's work attracted new critical approaches in the 1990s which have engendered new, more accurate ways of valuing and understanding Farrell's work. One important reason concerns the proper attention that began to be given to Farrell's relationship with and representation of Ireland. Displacing Farrell from the inaccurate position of a British writer, Margaret Scanlan's 1990 study of history and politics in postwar British fiction situates Farrell as an 'Anglo-Irish novelist' and explores *Troubles* alongside Elizabeth Bowen's novel *The Last September* (1929).[11] Scanlan argues that Farrell's representation of the Anglo-Irish Ascendancy 'is ironic where Bowen is elegiac', and points out the important political gesture of including Ireland in a trilogy of novels about British colonialism. Although, as we have seen previously, Scanlan was concerned with the representation of the Catholic Irish, her argument reveals the critical and ironic vision of Ireland in *Troubles* which makes it impossible to regard Farrell as a colonial nostalgic or naïve realist. More recently, Glenn Hooper has written expertly upon the ways in which *Troubles* offers a sensitive critique of colonialism in Ireland while signalling the decline of the British Empire on a global scale. As he concludes, Farrell 'declare[s] the road to Irish independence as the beginning of the end for empire'.[12]

Hooper's elegant and skilful essay draws on the insights of Irish and postcolonial studies. It evidences the fruitful ways in which postcolonial approaches to Farrell's work have produced important new readings which amend much of the prevailing criticism of the 1980s. A new field of cultural enquiry, postcolonial studies became increasingly influential by the early 1990s. In contrast to criticism of Commonwealth literature, postcolonial critics admitted (very properly) Ireland to their field of study. They were especially keen to explore the ways that literary texts confirmed or contested the continuation of colonial attitudes and assumptions – 'colonial discourses', in the new critical parlance. Postcolonial criticism also recognized a relationship between literary innovation and political critique, and often suggested that the experimental elements of postcolonial writing had a subversive intent in challenging the received cultural forms of colonizing countries. The Empire Trilogy appeared very differently when approached in the context of postcolonial studies: the link between Farrell's ironical, parodic style and anti-colonial critique appears much more visible.

Postcolonial approaches enabled a way out of crude assessments of Farrell's ideological sympathies as glibly 'Eurocentric' or naïvely complicit with colonial attitudes. It was not simply the case that his fiction was either 'for' or 'against' Empire. Rather, the ambivalent and occasionally contradictory currents in Farrell's writing evidenced both the possibilities and the limits of his particular position, inside, but not fully of, the culture of colonialism. In a 1994 essay on *The Siege of Krishnapur* I attempted to read the novel with the insights of postcolonial studies, and suggested that Farrell parodied the symbolic resources of colonial discourses in an attempt to critique their authority, even if he could not always give voice to the colonized Indians.[13]

Judie Newman's 1995 study of intertextuality in postcolonial fiction, *The Ballistic Bard*, takes its title from the incident in *The Siege of Krishnapur* when Shakespeare's head is fired from a cannon. For Newman, Farrell's work can be thought of as exemplary of much postcolonial writing in its attention to the complicity between culture and imperialism: 'Farrell reminds us that the study of postcolonial literature sheds light not merely on the object of study itself but also on the means by which English literature has been – and continues to be – shaped, inviting us to speculate on the relation between postcolonial literature and its predecessors'.[14] Rescuing Farrell from dismissal as elegiac for Empire, postcolonial approaches to Farrell have productively exposed the subversive and sober critique of colonialism which underwrites the often comical and absurd representation of Farrell's British colonial characters.

The late 1990s saw a gathering of significant critical work about Farrell. In particular, two important books appeared which offered a wide-ranging and in-depth discussion of Farrell's novels, often building upon and adding to the new insights brought by the critical approaches of the 1990s. Ralph Crane and Jennifer Livett's *Troubled Pleasures: The Fiction of J. G. Farrell* (1997) was the first full-length study since Ronald Binns's. It offers a detailed, imaginative and exhaustive exploration of each of Farrell's novels, including the early fiction. Crane and Livett demonstrate the complexity of Farrell's metafictional and intertextual rendering of Empire in particular, the growing influence of his Marxist sympathies, and his commitment to contesting the aims and attitudes of Empire.

In 1999 Crane edited *J. G. Farrell: The Critical Grip*, which brought together twelve literary scholars whose essays ranged diversely across the entirety of Farrell's œuvre. The image of Farrell which emerges from these essays is very different to the one gleaned from 1980s accounts of his work. Ronald Tamplin argues that *Troubles* can 'take its place within the Irish [literary] canon, some post-colonial recompense for all those Irish writers cannibalised or suborned by "English literature"'.[15] Daniel Lea demonstrates the metafictional and parodic strategies at the heart of *The Siege of Krishnapur* and argues that the novel, perhaps in a postmodernist vein, 'discloses the textualised labyrinth which constitutes our knowledge of the past and of our own self-realisation'.[16] Paul Smethurst reveals the affinities of *The Singapore Grip* with the work of more recent writers, Timothy Mo and Graham Swift, and demonstrates how their representations of history work to relocate historiographical narratives beyond limits of colonial vision.[17] As the range of such fertile readings show, the particularities of Farrell's ambiguous relationship with Britain and Ireland, his innovative style, and his critical and subversive purposes are now firmly installed on the critical agenda. The notion that Farrell's work looks backwards, in both form and content, has hopefully been discredited, and more thoughtful, patient, and sensitive critical encounters with his writing have superseded the earlier, often unsubtle, critical views of his achievement.

As if to demonstrate the establishment of Farrell's reputation as a writer of significance, in 1999 Lavinia Greacen's biography, *J. G. Farrell: The Making of a Writer*, was published. Meticulously researched and sensitively written, Greacen renders a full portrait of Farrell's life and reveals the complex relationship between the writer and his work. A deeply friendly and affection man, yet deliberately solitary— he never married and lived alone throughout his adult life – Farrell's commitment to writing became his greatest priority. As the poet Derek Mahon records in his foreword to Greacen's book, he was in many ways a man of contradictions: 'Ascetic epicurean, gregarious solitary, aristocrat of the spirit'.[18]

Indeed, if critics have not always valued Farrell's work then his fellow writers have often understood its significance; and to a certain extent Farrell's posthumous reputation has been maintained by writers. Derek Mahon's important poem 'A Disused Shed in County Wexford' is dedicated to Farrell, while Farrell's friend Margaret Drabble bases one of her fictional characters, Stephen Cox, on Farrell in her novel *The Gates of Ivory* (1991). At various public readings I have heard writers such as Giles Foden and Kazuo Ishiguro praise Farrell's contribution to the novel. On a visit to the University of Leeds in 1997, the novelist Amitav Ghosh told me that he considered Farrell to be one of the best writers about India. At the beginning of a new century, Farrell's place in literary history seems much more secure than it did in the years immediately after his death. For example, between 2002 and 2005, *The New York Review of Books* republished the Empire Trilogy with new introductions by John Banville, Pankaj Mishra and Derek Mahon.

'One day we shall vanish. But for the moment how lovely we are!' (*T* 329). Farrell's untimely death cruelly cut short the life and work of a unique and important writer. And although his work has at times seemed in danger of vanishing from sight – the early novels remain out of print, while the Empire Trilogy has often been passed over by those who have narrated the history of the twentieth-century novel – his mature writing has lasted far beyond the moment of its appearance and is now readily enjoyed and explored by an ever-growing circle of readers. To a degree Farrell's death will always inflect his work with an added and poignant sense of melancholy and loss. But like the Human Condition, fleeing besieged Singapore on a boat, Farrell's work endures – a fitting legacy, perhaps, for a writer whose life and work were so often concerned with survival.

Notes

CHAPTER 1. INTRODUCTION: 'FANCIFUL TALES'

1. The full text of the letter is available online at http://www.ny books.com/articles/8125 (accessed 21 September 2005).
2. Malcolm Dean, 'Grip of Empire', *Guardian*, 13 September 1978, 10.
3. John Spurling, 'Unlucky Jim ... ', *Observer Review*, 15 August 1999, 11.
4. See John McLeod, 'J. G. Farrell and Post-Imperial Fiction' in *J. G. Farrell: The Critical Grip*, ed. by Ralph Crane (Dublin: Four Courts Press, 1999), 178–195.
5. See Lavinia Greacen, *J. G. Farrell: The Making of a Writer* (London: Bloomsbury, 1999). Greacen's marvellous biography is required reading for all Farrell enthusiasts. Much of the information I provide about Farrell's life throughout this book is directly indebted to Greacen's meticulous research.
6. John Palliser, 'J. G. Farrell and the wisdom of comedy', *Literary Review*, 15–18 October 1979, 14.
7. Caroline Moorehead, 'Writing in the dark, and not a detail missed', *The Times*, 9 September 1978, 12.
8. Moorehead, 'Writing in the dark, and not a detail missed', 12.
9. 'J. G. Farrell' in *Bookmarks*, ed. by Frederick Raphael (London: Quartet, 1975), 49–52.
10. Ronald Binns, *J. G. Farrell* (Methuen: London and New York, 1986), 23.
11. Brigid Allen, 'A Feline Friend: Memories of J. G. Farrell (1935–1979)', *London Magazine* 32 (April–May 1992), 64–75 (75). Ralph Crane and Jennifer Livett ingenuously respond to Farrell's choice of 'pyjamas' in this remark in their perceptive study, *Troubled Pleasures: The Fiction of J. G. Farrell* (Dublin: Four Courts Press, 1997), 83.

CHAPTER 2. THE EARLY NOVELS

1. For example, like the Algerian town of Oran in Camus's *La Peste* (1947) the weather in Saint Guilhelm is unbearably hot. Oran is also mentioned briefly in a radio news broadcast which reports two explosions there.
2. Michael C. Prusse has convincingly argued that the encounter between Sayer and Regan specifically fictionalizes the famous conflict between Jean-Paul Sartre and Albert Camus. See Michael C. Prusse, *'Tomorrow is Another Day': The Fictions of James Gordon Farrell* (Tübingen: Francke, 1997), 40–41.
3. In an interview with Farrell in 1978, Caroline Moorehead remarked that 'He now rejects [*A Man From Elsewhere*] to the point of fantasizing that one day he will buy up every remaining copy and pulp it'. See Caroline•Moorehead, 'Writing in the dark, and not a detail missed', *Guardian*, 9 September 1978, 12. The novel has remained out of print for many years and, at the time of writing, copies are virtually impossible to find.
4. Ralph Crane and Jennifer Livett, *Troubled Pleasures: The Fiction of J. G. Farrell* (Dublin: Four Courts Press, 1997), 39–41. The quotation from Beckett can be found in Samuel Beckett, *The Beckett Trilogy: Molloy, Malone Dies, The Unnamable* (London: Picador, 1979 [1959]), 382.
5. See Michael C. Prusse, *'Tomorrow is Another Day': The Fictions of James Gordon Farrell*, 64–65.
6. Ralph Crane, 'Introduction' to *J. G. Farrell: The Critical Grip*, ed. by Ralph Crane (Dublin: Four Courts Press, 1999), 9–18 (10).
7. Both Michael C. Prusse's book and Ralph Crane and Jennifer Livett's study of Farrell pay patient and expert attention to the earlier novels. In addition, Chris Ackerly has written excellently on these texts in his essay 'A Fox in the Dongeon: the Presence of Malcolm Lowry in the Early Fiction of J. G. Farrell' in *J. G. Farrell: The Critical Grip*, ed. by Ralph Crane, 36–47. Lavinia Greacen's recent biography of Farrell, *J. G. Farrell: The Making of a Writer* (London: Bloomsbury, 1999), has thrown much valuable light on the early novels.
8. Ronald Binns, *J. G. Farrell* (London and New York: Methuen, 1986), 38.

CHAPTER 3. IRELAND, 1919–1921

1. Neil McEwan, *Perspective in British Historical Fiction Today* (London

and Basingstoke: Macmillan, 1987), 130.
2. For a discussion of the significance of parody in postmodern fiction, see Linda Hutcheon's books *A Theory of Parody: The Teachings of Twentieth Century Art-forms* (New York and London: Methuen, 1985) and *A Poetics of Postmodernism: History, Fiction, Politics* (London and New York: Routledge, 1988). Daniel Lea has made an important and convincing case for Farrell as a postmodern writer in his fine study *J. G. Farrell: Towards a Postmodern Fiction* (Royal Holloway College, University of London: unpublished PhD dissertation, 1996).
3. Tony Gould, 'The Man from Elsewhere', *New Society*, 28 April 1983, 147–148 (147).
4. 'J. G. Farrell Comments' in *Contemporary Novelists*, ed. by James Vinson (London: St. James Press: 1970), 399. Farrell's comment is also quoted in full in McEwan, *Perspective in British Historical Fiction Today*, 125.
5. Farrell's remark can be found in George Brock, 'Epitaph for the Empire', *Observer Magazine*, 24 September 1978, 73, 75.
6. Jacqueline Genet (ed.), *The Big House in Ireland: Reality and Representation* (Co. Kerry/Maryland: Barnes and Noble, 1991), ix.
7. Spenser's views on Ireland are usefully explored by Ciaran Brady in her essay 'The Road to the View: On the Decline of Reform Thought in Tudor Ireland' in *Spenser and Ireland: An Interdisciplinary Perspective*, ed. by Patricia Coughlin (Cork: Cork University Press, 1989), 25–45.
8. Brigid Allen, 'A Feline Friend: Memories of J. G. Farrell (1935–1979)' in *London Magazine*, 32 (1, 2), 1992, 64–75 (75).
9. Robert J. C. Young, *Postcolonialism: An Historical Introduction* (Oxford: Blackwell, 2001), 2.
10. Glenn Hooper, 'Troublesome Tales: J. G. Farrell and the Decline of Empire' in *Irish and Postcolonial Writing: History, Theory, Practice*, ed. by Glenn Hooper and Colin Graham (Basingstoke: Palgrave, 2002), pp. 222–249 (234).
11. See the account of the IRA's tactics in Robert Kee, *Ireland. A History*, revised edition (London: Abacus, 1995), 179–189.
12. Margaret Scanlan, *Traces of Another Time: History and Politics in Postwar British Fiction* (Princeton: Princeton University Press, 1990), 61

CHAPTER 4. INDIA, 1857 & 1871

1. Malcolm Dean, 'An Insight Job', *Guardian*, 1 September 1973, 11.
2. It has become increasingly unfashionable and problematic to use the term 'Mutiny' when discussing the events of 1857; many

contemporary historians and critics of India use the phrase 'the first war of independence' as a way of challenging the representation of the 1857 uprising in colonialist historiography. For reasons of space I shall stick to the one-word term 'Mutiny', and also because Farrell was challenging the 'Mutiny novel' in particular; but I do so while remaining fully cognizant of its troubling associations which I do not endorse.
3. Malcolm Dean, 'An Insight Job', 11.
4. Peter Morey, *Fictions of India: Narrative and Power* (Edinburgh: Edinburgh University Press, 2000), 110.
5. Christopher Hibbert, *The Great Mutiny: India 1857* (Harmondsworth: Penguin, 1978), 55. Hibbert's account of the causes, progress and consequences of the conflict is highly recommended.
6. Denis Judd, *Empire: The British Imperial Experience from 1765 to the Present* (HarperCollins: London, 1996), 67.
7. Jenny Sharpe 'The Unspeakable Limits of Rape: Colonial Violence and Counter-Insurgency' in *Colonial Discourse and Post-Colonial Theory*, ed. by Patrick Williams and Laura Chrisman (London and New York: Harvester Wheatsheaf, 1993), 221–243 (227).
8. Ralph Crane and Jennifer Livett, *Troubled Pleasures*, 83–84.
9. S. D. Singh, *Novels on the Indian Mutiny* (New Delhi: Arnold-Heinemann, 1973), 183.
10. Homi K. Bhabha, *The Location of Culture* (London and New York: Routledge, 1994), 86.
11. Francis B. Singh, 'Progress and History in J.G. Farrell's *The Siege of Krishnapur*', *Chandrabhaga*, 2, 1979, 23–39 (37).
12. John Spurling's appreciation of Farrell published alongside *The Hill Station* attempts to predict the novel's conclusions by making reference to Farrell's notes. See *HS*, 155–177.
13. See Ralph Crane and Jennifer Livett, *Troubled Pleasures*, 123.

CHAPTER 5. SINGAPORE, 1937–1942

1. Timothy Mo, 'Magpie Man', *New Statesman*, 15 September 1978, 337–338 (337).
2. Lawrence James, *The Rise and Fall of the British Empire* (London: Little, Brown and Company, 1994), 491.
3. Lavinia Greacen, *J. G. Farrell: The Making of a Writer* (London: Bloomsbury, 1999), 333.
4. Paul Smethurst, 'Post-Imperial Topographies: the Undergrounding of History in J. G. Farrell's *The Singapore Grip*, Timothy Mo's *An Insular Possession*, and Graham Swift's *Waterland*' in *J. G. Farrell: The Critical Grip*, ed. by Ralph Crane (Dublin: Four Courts Press, 1999),

112–127 (112).
5. I am following here the thinking of Mikhail Bakhtin, who proposes that the carnivalesque attempts to challenge 'all that is high, spiritual, ideal, abstract' by lowering it to the level of 'earth and body', especially through a focus upon and celebration of excrescent bodily functions. See Mikhail Bakhtin, *Rabelais and his World*, trans. by H. Iwolsky (Bloomington: Indiana University Press, 1984), 20.
6. Lavinia Greacen, *J. G. Farrell*, 307. Farrell used his prize money to travel extensively in Singapore, Malaya and Vietnam as part of his research for the novel.

CHAPTER 6. CRITICAL LEGACY

1. Bernard Bergonzi, *The Situation of the Novel*, second edition (London and Basingstoke: Macmillan, 1979), 236.
2. John Banville, 'Introduction' to J. G. Farrell, *Troubles* (1970; New York: New York Review of Books, 2002), v–ix (vi).
3. Bergonzi, *The Situation of the Novel*, 235.
4. Bergonzi, *The Situation of the Novel*, 229.
5. Neil McEwan, *Perspective in British Historical Fiction Today* (London and Basingstoke: Macmillan, 1987), 130.
6. Malcolm Bradbury, *No, Not Bloomsbury* (London: Arena, 1987), 101. A more gracious and thoughtful response to Farrell is found in Malcolm Bradbury, *The Modern British Novel* (1983; London: Penguin, 1994), 382.
7. Ralph Crane and Jennifer Livett, *Troubled Pleasures: The Fiction of J. G. Farrell* (Dublin: Four Courts Press, 1997), 99.
8. Randall Stevenson, *The British Novel Since the Thirties* (London: Batsford, 1986).
9. Patricia Waugh, *Harvest of the Sixties: English Literature and its Background 1960–1990* (Oxford: Oxford University Press, 1995), 202.
10. Crane and Livett, *Troubled Pleasures*, 14.
11. Margaret Scanlan, *Traces of Another Time: History and Politics in Postwar British Fiction* (Princeton: Princeton University Press, 1990), 40. Bowen was an admirer of *Troubles*.
12. Glenn Hooper, 'Troublesome Tales: J. G. Farrell and the Decline of Empire' in *Irish and Postcolonial Writing: History, Theory, Practice*, ed. by Glenn Hooper and Colin Graham (Basingstoke: Palgrave, 2002), 222–49 (245).
13. See John McLeod, 'Exhibiting Empire in J. G. Farrell's *The Siege of Krishnapur*', *Journal of Commonwealth Literature*, 29:2 (1994), 117–132.
14. Judie Newman, *The Ballistic Bard: Postcolonial Fictions* (London:

Arnold, 1995), 2.
15. Ronald Tamplin, '*Troubles* and the Irish Tradition' in *J. G. Farrell: The Critical Grip*, ed. by Ralph Crane (Dublin: Four Courts Press, 1999), 48–64 (64).
16. Daniel Lea, 'Parodic Strategy and the Mutiny Romance in *The Siege of Krishnapur*', in Crane (ed.), *J. G. Farrell*, 65–79 (78).
17. See Paul Smethurst, 'Post-Imperial Topographies: the Undergrounding of History in J. G. Farrell's *The Singapore Grip*, Timothy Mo's *An Insular Possession*, and Graham Swift's *Waterland*' in Crane (ed.), *J. G. Farrell*, 112–127.
18. Lavina Greacen, *J. G. Farrell: The Making of a Writer* (London: Bloomsbury, 1999), vxii.

Select Bibliography

For a full bibliography of reviews of Farrell's novels, as well as his published non-fiction, see Ralph J. Crane, 'J. G. Farrell: A Bibliography of Primary and Secondary Sources' in *J. G. Farrell: The Critical Grip*, ed. by Ralph J. Crane (Dublin: Four Courts Press, 1999), 196-210. Farrell's papers are held at Trinity College Dublin, Ireland (Mss.9128–60: Papers of James Gordon Farrell (1935–1979)).

PUBLISHED FICTION BY FARRELL (first editions, by date of publication)

A Man From Elsewhere (London: New Authors, 1963).
The Lung (London: Hutchinson, 1965).
A Girl in the Head (London, Jonathan Cape, 1967).
Troubles (London: Jonathan Cape, 1970).
The Siege of Krishnapur (London: Weidenfeld and Nicolson, 1973).
'The Pussycat Who Fell in Love with the Suitcase', *Atlantis* 6 (1973–74), 6–10 [short story].
The Singapore Grip (London: Weidenfeld and Nicolson, 1978).
The Hill Station: an unfinished novel and an Indian Diary (with Two Appreciations and a Personal Memoir), ed. by John Spurling (London: Weidenfeld and Nicolson, 1981).

BIOGRAPHY, MEMOIRS AND INTERVIEWS

Allen, Brigid, 'A Feline Friend: Memories of J. G. Farrell (1935–1979)', *London Magazine* 32 (April–May 1992), 64–75.
Brock, George, 'Epitaph for the Empire', *Observer Magazine*, 24 September 1978, 73–75.
Dean, Malcolm, 'An Insight Job', *Guardian*, 1 September 1973, 11.
—— 'Grip of Empire', *Guardian*, 13 September 1978, 10.

Greacen, Lavinia, *J. G. Farrell: The Making of a Writer* (London: Bloomsbury, 1999).
Moorehead, Caroline, 'Writing in the dark, and not a detail missed', *The Times*, 9 September 1978, 12.
O'Toole, Bridget, 'Not a Crumb, Not a Wrinkle: J. G. Farrell at Work', *Irish Studies Review*, 12 (1995), 27–30.
Spurling, John, 'Unlucky Jim ', *Observer Review*, 15 August 1999.

SCHOLARLY CRITICISM

Bergonzi, Bernard, *The Situation of the Novel*, second edition (London and Basingstoke: Macmillan, 1979).
Binns, Ronald, *J. G. Farrell* (Methuen: London and New York, 1986).
Bristow-Smith, Lawrence, ' "Tomorrow is Another Day": The Essential J. G. Farrell', *Critical Quarterly*, 25.2 (1983), 45–52.
Crane, Ralph, and Livett, Jennifer, *Troubled Pleasures: The Fiction of J. G. Farrell* (Dublin: Four Courts Press, 1997).
Crane, Ralph J. (ed.), *J. G. Farrell: The Critical Grip*, (Dublin: Four Courts Press, 1999).
Crane, Ralph J. ' "J.G. Farrell, an Australian": or, The Trope of Australia in the Fiction of J.G. Farrell', *Journal of Commonwealth Literature*, 34.2 (1999), 47–60.
Donnelly, Brian, 'The Big House in the Recent Irish Novel', *Studies: Irish Quarterly Review* 14 (1975), 133–142.
Ferns, Chris, ' "First as tragedy, then as farce": J. G. Farrell's Retelling of History', *Dalhousie Review* 67 (1987), 161–172.
Hartveit, Lars, 'The "jolting passage over the switched points of history" and the Experience of Dislocation in J. G. Farrell's *The Singapore Grip*', *English Studies: A Journal of English Language and Literature*, 70.6 (1989), 566–580.
—— 'The Carnivalistic Impulse in J.G. Farrell's *Troubles*', *English Studies: A Journal of English Language and Literature*, 73.5 (1992), 444–457.
—— 'The Imprint of Recorded Events in the Narrative Form of J. G. Farrell's *The Siege of Krishnapur*', *English Studies: A Journal of English Language and Literature*, 74.5 (1993), 451–469.
Gould, Tony, 'The Man from Elsewhere', *New Society*, 28 April 1983, 147–148.
Hooper, Glenn, 'Troublesome Tales: J. G. Farrell and the Decline of Empire' in *Irish and Postcolonial Writing: History, Theory, Practice*, ed. by Glenn Hooper and Colin Graham (Basingstoke: Palgrave, 2002), 222–249.
McEwan, Neil, *Perspective in British Historical Fiction Today* (London and Basingstoke: Macmillan, 1987).

McLeod, John, 'Exhibiting Empire in J. G. Farrell's *The Siege of Krishnapur'*, *Journal of Commonwealth Literature*, 29:2 (1994).

McPhail, Fiona, 'Major and Majestic: J. G. Farrell's *Troubles*' in *The Big House in Ireland: Reality and Representation*, ed. by Jacqueline Genet (Co. Kerry: Brandon), 243–252.

Morey, Peter, *Fictions of India: Narrative and Power* (Edinburgh: Edinburgh University Press, 2000).

Newman, Judie, *The Ballistic Bard: Postcolonial Fictions* (London: Arnold, 1995).

John Palliser, 'J. G. Farrell and the wisdom of comedy', *Literary Review*, 15–18 (October 1979).

Prusse, Michael C., *'Tomorrow is Another Day': The Fictions of James Gordon Farrell* (Tübingen: Francke, 1997).

Rignall, J. M., 'Walter Scott, J. G. Farrell, and the Fictions of Empire', *Essays in Criticism* 41 (1991), 11–27.

Scanlan, Margaret, *Traces of Another Time: History and Politics in Postwar British Fiction* (Princeton: Princeton University Press, 1990).

Singh, Francis B., 'Progress and History in J.G. Farrell's *The Siege of Krishnapur'*, *Chandrabhaga*, 2, 1979, 23–39.

Waugh, Patricia, *Harvest of the Sixties: English Literature and its Background 1960–1990* (Oxford: Oxford University Press, 1995).

Index

A Girl in the Head 7, 24–33, 37, 54
A Man From Elsewhere 6, 11–17, 23, 25, 32–3
Allen, Brigid 46

Baldwin, James 1
Bantry Bay 2
Banville, John 97, 104
Beckett, Samuel 17
Bergonzi, Bernard 97–9
Bhabha, Homi 72
'Big House' novel 34, 41, 56
Binns, Ronald 5, 32, 100, 102
Bowen, Elizabeth 41, 101
Bradbury, Malcolm 97, 99
Brasenose College, Oxford 5
Britain 4, 6, 35
British Empire – *see* Empire

Camus, Albert 11
Canada 5, 18
China 82, 86, 93
colonialism 1–2, 6, 8, 10, 39, 44, 55, 58, 60–3, 72, 83, 88, 90–2, 95, 98–102
Commonwealth literature 99, 101
Connor, Steven 97
Conrad, Joseph 4
Crane, Ralph 17, 32, 63, 76, 99–100, 102–3

Deane, Malcolm 56
Desai, Anita 99
Drabble, Margaret 1, 3, 72, 104

Edgeworth, Maria 41
Empire 2, 6, 7, 8, 9, 10, 35, 38–41, 43, 46–9, 55, 61–2, 69, 73, 77, 80–1, 83–4, 86–92, 94–5, 97–100, 102
Empire Trilogy 2, 6, 8, 10, 16, 24, 30, 32–4, 38, 46, 48, 52, 55, 60, 73, 76, 79, 80–2, 84, 86, 88, 91, 96–7, 99–100, 104

Foden, Giles 10, 104
Forster, E. M. 44
Fowles, John 98
France 6, 11, 40
Freud, Sigmund 77

Genet, Jacqueline 41
Ghosh, Amitav 2, 104
Gould, Tony 36
Greacen, Lavinia 3, 10, 83, 103
Great Exhibition 58, 61, 69

Hibbert, Christopher 57
Hill Station, The 10, 30 73–8
historical novel 7, 9, 36–7, 80
Hong Kong 80
Hooper, Glenn 49, 101
Hughes, Richard 4

India 8, 9, 10, 47, 56–8, 61–4, 67, 69–74, 86, 104
Indian Diary 71–2
Ireland 3, 4, 7, 8, 34–6, 38, 43–4, 46–7, 51–4, 99–101, 103
Ishiguro, Kazuo 2, 104
Italy 47

INDEX

Japan 8, 81, 95
Johnson, B. S. 98
Judd, Denis 57

Kipling, Rudyard 56
Kneale, Matthew 10

Lea, Daniel 3, 103
Livett, Jennifer 17, 63, 76, 99–100, 102
Loti, Pierre 4
Lung, The 5, 6, 17–28, 32–3, 75–6, 83, 93, 96

McEwan, Neil 34, 98
Mahon, Derek 103–4
Malaya 8, 86, 92, 95–6
Marx, Karl 77, 83
Master, John 56
Mesopotamia 47
Mishra, Pankaj 104
Mistry, Rohinton 10
Mo, Timothy 2, 10, 79, 100, 103
Moorehead, Caroline 4
Morey, Peter 56
'Mutiny novel' 63–4

Newman, Judie 102
Ngugi wa Thiong'o 1, 2, 10, 99

O'Brien, Edna 1

Palliser, John 3
Phillips, Caryl 100
Pinter, Harold 1
polio 2, 5, 6, 17
postcolonial 2, 8, 48, 66, 88, 93, 100–2
postmodern 35
postmodernist 51–2, 103
Pynchon, Thomas 98

Roth, Philip 1
Rushdie, Salman 2, 100
Russia 47, 93

Sartre, Jean-Paul 11, 37
Scanlan, Margaret 53, 101
Scott, Paul 44, 99
Sharpe, Jenny 63
Siege of Krishnapur, The 1, 6, 8, 10, 23, 27, 30, 56–73, 75, 77, 80, 85, 94, 97, 102–3
Singapore 8, 9, 78–94, 104
Singapore Grip, The 2, 8, 9, 10, 30, 46, 73, 75–97, 103
Singh, Frances B. 72
Singh, S. D. 64
Smethurst, Paul 84, 103
South Africa 47
Spenser, Edmund 44
Spurling, John 2, 3, 73
Stevenson, Randall 99
Swift, Graham 103

Tamplin, Ronald 103
Taylor, D. J. 97
Tolstoy, Leo 4, 38
transnational 48–9
Trilogy – *see* Empire Trilogy
Troubles 1, 2, 6, 7, 8, 22, 23, 30, 34–56, 58, 60–1, 70–1, 73, 75, 80, 82, 85, 95–7, 100, 103

United States 7, 81
University of Leeds 104

Vietnam 9

Waugh, Patricia 97, 99
White, Patrick 99

Young, Robert 49

Printed in the United Kingdom
by Lightning Source UK Ltd.
132345UK00001B/133-204/A